the
extra
hour

Powerful Productivity
Techniques to Create
More Time in Your Day

WILL DECLAIR
BAO DINH
JEROME DUMONT

1 3 5 7 9 10 8 6 4 2

Virgin Books, an imprint of Ebury Publishing,
20 Vauxhall Bridge Road,
London SW1V 2SA

Virgin Books is part of the Penguin Random House group of companies
whose addresses can be found at global.penguinrandomhouse.com

Penguin
Random House
UK

First published in France by Jerome Dumont in 2018
This edition first published in the United Kingdom by
Virgin Books in 2020

www.penguin.co.uk

A CIP catalogue record for this book is available from
the British Library

ISBN 9780753557907

Typeset in 10.2/15.43 Georgia Pro
by Integra Software Services Pvt. Ltd, Pondicherry

Printed and bound in Great Britain by Clays Ltd, Elcograf S.p.A.

Penguin Random House is committed to a sustainable future for
our business, our readers and our planet. This book is made from
Forest Stewardship Council® certified paper.

MIX
Paper from
responsible sources
FSC
www.fsc.org   FSC® C018179

If you're interested in helping your coworkers or employees win back an extra hour every day, visit www.extrahourbook.com/enterprise or write to us at hey@extrahourbook.com for discounted bulk corporate orders and we will point you in the right direction!

Throughout the book, we've cited a bunch of very helpful tools. Now, productivity tools are evolving faster than the print rate of this book. If you can't find some of the tools we mention in this book, it's probably because they have been replaced by more effective tools or have changed names. But we won't let you down, we are keeping an up-to-date list of tools at www.extrahourbook.com/tools.

Contents

Contents

For all those who type with one finger,
and for those they drive crazy.

Before we get started ...

LIFE IS SHORT

First up, a diagram, or rather a series of circles.

Each circle represents a month of your life.

For most, it's hard to think of life as anything but an infinite series of months, each one spilling into the next. But here they all are: the months of your life, mapped out one by one. If you're 30, 60 or 90 years old, here's exactly where you stand on the diagram.

Each line = 36 months (or 3 years)

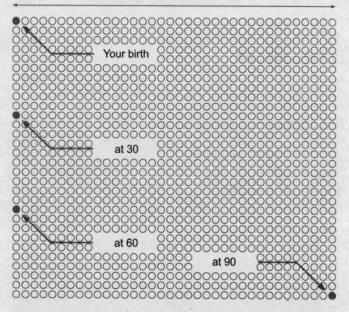

Your birth

at 30

at 60

at 90

The above infographic by Tim Urban, the author behind the fantastic *WaitButWhy* blog demonstrates one thing: that life is a finite resource, and far too short to waste.

In this context, productivity is not the end in itself, but a means to a better overall existence. By spending as little time as possible on uninspiring, tedious tasks, we can spend more on what really makes us happy.

In other words, mastering productivity can help us live more fully. For you, that could mean:

> Heading off on an adventure somewhere you've always wanted to go.
> Enjoying long, meaningful conversations with friends over dinner.
> Coming home early in the evenings to spend time with your kids.
> Working on the projects that truly inspire you.

THE PROGRESS PARADOX – WHY ARE WE WORKING MORE?

Three centuries ago, you'd need to work for about six hours in order to pay for the quantity of candles required to see you through a reading of this book. Today, thanks to rising revenue and technological advances that have dramatically lowered the price of lightbulbs,[1] you now only need to work half a second to get the same amount of light.

Since the start of the Industrial Revolution, output efficiency has risen considerably across most economic

---

[1]   Matt Ridley, *The Rational Optimist* (2010), numbers from the work of the economist William Nordhaus.

sectors. As a result, the number of hours worked per person has dropped significantly since then – particularly among blue-collar workers.

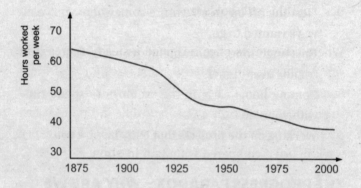

The average working week of a North American/Western European blue-collar worker[2]

In 1930, the economist John Maynard Keynes predicted that with continuing advances in productivity, the twenty-first century would give rise to a 15-hour working week for all.

And yet this never happened. In fact, in recent years, progress in productivity has pretty much come to a halt.

The Third Industrial Revolution sees rapid growth in the IT and communications sectors. But following an initial

2 Michael Huberman & Chris Minns, 'The times they are not changin': Days and hours of work in Old and New Worlds, 1870–2000.' *Explorations in Economic History*, 44 (2007): 538–567.

spike in productivity, growth slowed to such an extent that between 2010 and 2016, productivity in North America and Western Europe increased by just 0.5 per cent per year.[3] As far back as 1987, Nobel Prize-winning economist Robert Solow observed that 'you can see the computer age everywhere but in the productivity statistics', and this still holds true.

Where economists once imagined a steady decrease in working hours, the average working week for a full-time employee in the US has remained virtually unchanged since 2001 at just over 47 hours,[4] while in France it has risen, with executives working on average 44.1 hours per week in 2011[5] compared with 42.6 in 2003.

These days, a laid-back lunch break is out of the question, and our workers are habitually underwater. Our friends work late into evenings and weekends, and the term *burnout* has become a standard part of our vocabulary. White-collar is the new blue-collar.

The introduction of machines successfully reduced the working week for blue-collar workers, but new

---

[3] McKinsey Global Institute, 'Solving the productivity puzzle: the role of demand and the promise of digitization' (February 2018).
[4] Source: Gallup Work and Education Surveys carried out in August each year.
[5] DARES survey of executives and academic professionals from competitive non-agricultural sectors.

technologies have not had the same benefits for their colleagues in the boardroom. Why?

It's a reasonable question. Whereas previous generations had little more than pens and paper to facilitate tasks, we now possess an impressive array of digital tools whose sole purpose is to make our jobs and lives easier, from streamlining tasks to full-on automating them.

One answer is that modern approaches to work actually make us less efficient. We waste too much time in pointless meetings, are endlessly interrupted in open-plan office spaces, and rely so heavily on digital technology that our smartphones, tablets and computers are constantly competing for our attention. Add in the constant stream of emails and text messages that endlessly disrupt our concentration, and it seems pretty clear that although we spend a lot of time *at* work, we don't actually get a whole lot of work done.

Our point here is that new technology should be used to liberate us from work, rather than tie us to it. We need to flip the roles in our relationship with digital technology and make it work for us, not the other way around. We should learn to harness the pressure we experience at work to motivate us, get organized, concentrate better, and work faster. By leaving the drudgery to digital technology, we can focus on the most creative and interesting aspects of our work – and of our lives.

HAPPY ARE THE LAZY

More than anything, productivity is a question of finding the right mindset. For us, that mindset boils down to a single motto: *embrace laziness*.

To clarify, we're not saying kick back and shirk your responsibilities, we're saying get strategic about your to-dos by looking for ways to sidestep as many low-value tasks as you possibly can. Basically, anytime you find yourself grinding away at a long, repetitive, or boring task, you should ask yourself how you might tweak the way you work to avoid having to do it again in the future. Admittedly, faced with all our more pressing day-to-day matters, making time to reflect on *how* we work isn't easy. What is, and always will be, is simply to stay on autopilot and continue doing as you've always done. A few examples:

> Putting up with the same pointless meetings each week instead of taking the time to re-prioritize your schedule once and for all.
> Wasting time on unimportant yet time-consuming tasks instead of training someone else to do them.
> Deleting unread promotional newsletters one by one instead of just unsubscribing from them altogether.

What we need to do is adopt an *investment mindset* whereby we put in the effort in the short-term to get results in the long-term. Basically, we should be thinking about our productivity the way a business would, and invest to succeed.

If a week goes by and you haven't made any tweaks to the way you work, you're probably not examining your habits with a critical-enough eye. It's crucial to embrace the idea of continuous improvement and place this investment mindset at the heart of your routine.

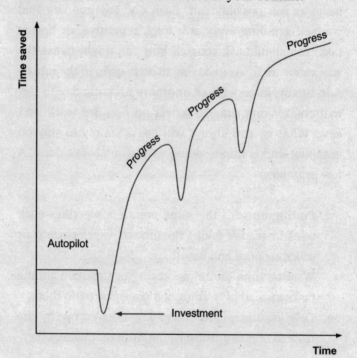

Fair warning: your gains will likely seem insignificant at first. A little tweak that makes you one per cent faster only saves you about 30 minutes over the course of a forty-hour week – hardly noticeable to you (or anyone around you, for that matter). But it's the snowball effect of these small improvements that will eventually make the difference. If every week, you can make a change that saves just one per cent of your time, then by the end of the year, a week's work will take you just 24 hours in total. By adopting this approach, you also stand to benefit from what economists call the Ratchet Effect, where each improvement creates so much value that a return to old ways seems almost inconceivable. To stay motivated, remind yourself that the greater your initial investments, the greater the future payoff.

And there you have the fundamental secret to super-charged productivity: implement a series of gradual improvements that eventually add up to an enormous difference.

Despite what some might like you to believe, extreme productivity isn't an innate gift. The people we know who finish work early, have a great family life and run successful projects on the side have invested time each and every day developing skills and implementing methods that allow them to be highly efficient. Here's a great example: a recent study[6] of 50,000 employees found that those who used Firefox or Chrome as their web browser consistently outperformed those with Internet Explorer or Safari. On average, Firefox and Chrome users reached their objectives 25 per cent faster than the latter group. The research team's explanation for this: those who take the time to seek out optimal browsers – as opposed to simply sticking with the computer's default options – are likely to be the kinds of people always on the lookout for ways to improve.

Invest time in improving yourself and your habits slowly but surely. Making a positive difference is achieved gradually. The results may be imperceptible at first, but don't be discouraged: one day you'll look back and be amazed by how far you've come.

HOW WE WROTE THIS BOOK IN A WEEKEND (MORE OR LESS)

When we – that's Bao, Jerome and Will – started out on our careers, we did what most people do: we worked late, we worked weekends, and we felt worn out. In college and at work, the focus is on learning technical

---

[6] The research carried out in 2015 by Cornerstone OnDemand looked at 50,000 candidates who applied for positions in a call center. The employees who used Firefox or Chrome reached the requisite customer satisfaction rating in 90 days as opposed to the 120 days it took the rest.

skills; oddly, it never occurs to anyone to teach us how to work effectively.

Gradually, the three of us became obsessed with finding ways to boost our productivity in order to spend the least amount of time possible on tedious tasks that wore us down, and more time on things that mattered to us. We started reading every book and blog we could on the subject of productivity and talked about it to everyone we knew, all the while testing out the different methods and approaches we'd picked up. Now, we're so productive that we spend the majority of our days sipping cocktails in the Bahamas.

Just kidding. But improving our effectiveness has enabled us to make a much greater impact at work and on our own projects in less time, which means that ultimately, we get to spend more time with family and friends and less with colleagues.

At some point, we realized we had accumulated enough research to fill a book. Before setting out to write it though, we decided to ask some entrepreneurs for help. What all the best startups share in common is that they've succeeded in creating maximum impact with both limited time and financial resources. From the point of view of a startup, working efficiently often means the difference between the life or slow death of the project. So for those seeking advice about managing time, startups are the perfect resource. After all, if you're looking for advice about managing a limited water supply, you're better off asking someone who lives in the desert rather than by a mountain stream.

We sent an email to all our entrepreneurial friends and contacts asking them a simple question: *what is the one thing that saves you the most time in your day-to-day life?* To be honest, we weren't expecting more than a few short replies, but we ended up with over 200 enthusiastic responses. And instead of conducting our conversations largely via email as we'd imagined, we were lucky enough to meet most entrepreneurs face to face, which meant we could really pick their brains. With our research gathered, we rented a car and drove to Jerome's house in Normandy for the weekend. Here, shut off from the rest of the world, we opened our laptops and started to type. By Sunday evening, we had our first draft.

Following the success of our book in France, we decided to write an international edition (which you now hold in your hands), adding to the original text with contributions from over 100 more entrepreneurs based all over the world. Among the 300 entrepreneurs who have contributed to this book, we are delighted to be able to include advice from the founders of BambooHR, Casper, Hired, Instacart, Made, MealPal, OnePlus, Product Hunt, Spotify, Techstars, Zoom, Zumper ... These new ideas have enriched our book with new perspectives on a wide range of subjects, from team management, to AI to connected speakers.

THE PRODUCTIVITY EQUATION

Self-help books have a tendency to dance around their main thesis rather than going straight to the point. With *The Extra Hour*, we have tried to keep ours as concise and actionable as possible. So let's dive in. Productivity follows a simple equation:

$$
\textbf{Work Completed}
$$

$$
=
$$

$$
\textbf{(Time Spent)}
$$
$$
\times
$$
$$
\textbf{(Intensity of Concentration)}
$$
$$
\times
$$
$$
\textbf{(Speed of Execution)}
$$

As far as we're concerned, to become super-productive, you must:

> Get organized: allocate enough time to do each job properly.
> Concentrate: give each task the focus it requires.
> Accelerate: get through each task as quickly and efficiently as possible.

These three skills form the pillars of this book, and we've dedicated one chapter to each.

The importance of each skill and their bearing on your work will depend largely on your role within a business or organization. In theory, the priority for a junior-level employee is production, so it follows that their main concern will be on learning to *concentrate* and *accelerate* each task. The task of proper time allocation is likely to fall to their manager, whose role, amongst others, is to help them *organize* their working day. Meanwhile, an exec must both *organize* time effectively and demonstrate a capacity to *concentrate* conducive to developing a long-term vision for the business (while resolving complex issues along the way). Whatever your particular role at work, it's never too early (nor too late!) to try and improve in each of these areas.

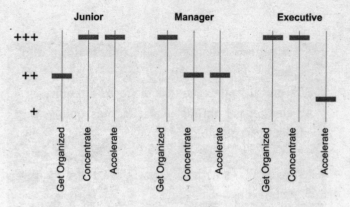

The key priorities for each position

One last thing: many of the techniques outlined in the first chapter (*Get organized*) are well-established and have been extensively tried and tested. The sheer number of entrepreneurs who endorse them testifies as much to their effectiveness as it does to the need for more detailed explanations than we've provided here. So just in case you want to dig a little further into a particular topic, we've provided you with the names of the authors along with references to their work.

Happy reading!

If you'd like to have your own personalized 'Your Life in Months' infographic made, send us an email at mylife@extrahourbook.com with your date of birth in the format yyyy-mm-dd in the subject.

CHAPTER 1

GET ORGANIZED

8,000 years passed between the Agricultural and Industrial Revolutions, 120 years between the first Industrial Revolution and the invention of the light bulb, 90 years between the invention of the light bulb and man's first trip to the moon, 22 years between the moonwalk and the invention of the internet, and nine years between the internet and DNA sequencing.

In other words, technology has never progressed faster than it does today. There's a term for this, coined by scientist and progress researcher Ray Kurzweil: The Law of Accelerating Returns. Kurzweil's law holds that because we build new technologies on the backs of existing ones, progress grows exponentially. Essentially, it's much easier to sequence DNA using a high-powered modern computer than the mechanical calculator Blaise Pascal invented in 1642.

It doesn't end there. Technology also spreads across the globe faster than ever before. It took 80 years for 80 per cent of the world to get access to telephone lines, 30 years for mobile phones, and only 10 for smartphones.

The future will surely see the rate of change accelerate further, particularly with the convergence of NBIC technologies

(Nanotechnology, Biotechnology, Information Technology and Cognitive Science).

Within this context, modern businesses must prepare themselves for sudden, monumental shifts in the landscape. Whether it occurs now or down the road, every industry will eventually have to reckon with some kind of disruption. Recently, it was the music industry with the arrival of streaming services, retail with Amazon, or hotels with Airbnb. In the not-too-distant future, automation will bring massive change to the automotive industry, nanotechnology will revolutionize health, and digitalization will transform the banking and insurance sectors. Seven of the top ten companies with the greatest global market value in 2018 – Apple, Alphabet, Microsoft, Amazon, Facebook, Alibaba, and Tencent – were completely unknown to the previous generation.

In a world of constantly-evolving priorities, businesses have been forced to shift the focus from the long term to the immediate. Ten-year strategic planning has given way to yearly or even quarterly concerns.

Employees too must be able to adapt to their company's constantly changing priorities. Whether it's the race to develop a product before a competitor, to update existing technologies in response to changing practices, or to tap into the potential of Blockchain and machine learning, each of us will face an ever-growing list of shifting tasks and projects to complete.

Within this whirlwind, the most important resource you have is your time, so the way you organize it is crucial. For this, you'll need to get organized and put a system in place to enhance your productivity. This chapter will help you do just that.

Get organized

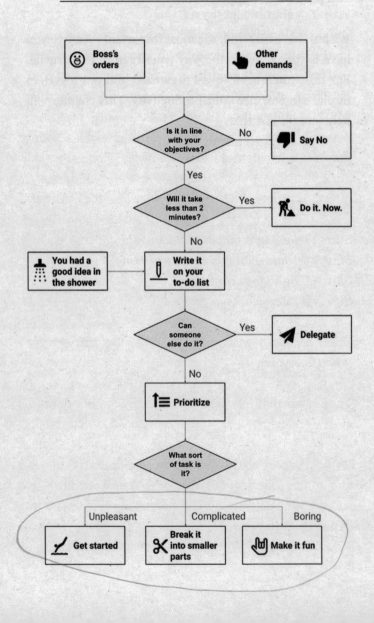

THE POWER OF NO

Why you should just say no

The definition of productivity is not 'doing lots of things'. Productivity is about strategically choosing your priorities and picking the battles that best line up with your objectives. Whatever your job, in your day-to-day life, you face an endless list of tasks, emails, meetings, demands from your boss, and so on. Your email account becomes a giant to-do list to which anyone can add anything at any time. If you say yes to everything asked of you, your day will be full before you've even started.

Sure, I'll look into that new partnership.
Sure, I'll come with you to that meeting.
Sure, I'll go to that conference.
Sure, I'll interview your friend.

There are two reasons why we have a tendency to say yes to everyone.

The first is that our personal objectives aren't defined clearly enough.

Without precise objectives, you become passively vulnerable to the countless demands placed on your time. In addition, the only measure of progress you have is how many hours you spend at the office, a fact that may lead you to prolong tasks longer than necessary. Taking back control of your schedule will mean getting proactive and clearly defining your goals. You should be able to provide a precise answer to the question 'what goal am I working towards today (or this quarter)?' at any given moment. This will then provide you with a framework to either accept or reject a given demand. Almost all the entrepreneurs we met could precisely identify their long and short-term goals.

The second reason we say yes so much is that we're afraid of letting people down.

We need to move past this way of thinking. In actuality, agreeing to something despite your reservations doesn't demonstrate your respect, and may in fact do the reverse. Doing something against your will or better judgement saps your motivation and makes you more likely to disappoint as a result. Take the time to politely decline, outlining your reasons for doing so. The person doing the asking will feel more respected in the long run.

The ability to say no becomes increasingly important as your career progresses and the demands placed on you grow. While your ability to take on new tasks stays largely the same, you'll find yourself having to turn down requests with increasing regularity. To give you some context, the founder of a highly successful startup we interviewed told us that for every 20 requests he receives, he'll turn down 19. It is absolutely crucial to weigh the pros and cons before you agree to something. For each yes you give, be prepared to say no many times over.

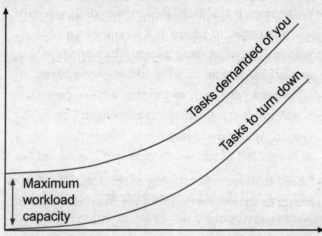

The Frequency Illusion: why it's important to keep your objectives in mind

Note: throughout the book, grey boxes like this one highlight subjects worth exploring and tools you might find useful.

Having a clear idea of your objectives will also help you recognize things that may be beneficial that crop up unintentionally, whether while chatting with colleagues, meeting a client or simply reading an article.

Without even realizing, we are incredibly selective when it comes to where and how we focus our attention. You've probably noticed the way something that's been on your mind suddenly seems to pop up all around you. Or how the moment we pick up a new term, everyone seems to be using it. Or how the second we decide to buy a new home, the world is suddenly full of real-estate agents. This is what behavioral psychologists refer to as 'The Frequency Illusion'. All the signs were already there, but they were filtered out by our brain in order to keep us focused on the task at hand. Having your goals in mind primes you to be on the lookout for any information or opportunities that may benefit you.

How to say no

Whatever happens, bear in mind that it's always better to say no and to explain your reasoning than to say yes to something you know you can't do – or can't do well. It's better to spend a minute turning someone down than an hour wasting time on a fruitless task. Here's an example of how you might gracefully turn down an invitation to lunch, as provided by one entrepreneur we spoke with.

'Hi Martin, thanks for reaching out. I'd have loved to have lunch with you, but I've been trying to condense my working days to free up a little more time for myself. If you have any specific questions, please email them over and I'll be more than happy to answer them for you.'

The opening line serves to keep the refusal friendly and non-personal (after all, you might end up meeting this person one day). The second part communicates that your no is final. It's important not to give an excuse that leaves the door open. Ideally, take the time to personalize your reply – it's always much nicer for the person you're responding to. Remember that you stand to lose more by agreeing to something you're unprepared for than you do by politely turning it down.

This holds even if it's your boss who's asking you to do something that seems like a waste of time, so don't be afraid to say no to him or her either. Explain your reasoning clearly and politely and try to anticipate any possible counter-arguments. A good superior will respect you all the more for having successfully made your point, and, of course, they stand to benefit too. The best managers encourage discussion within the workplace and will support those who demonstrate real conviction. Worst-case scenario, your manager will successfully convince you otherwise and you'll have found the motivation you need!

How to say no to meetings

Without a doubt, one of the most useful bits of advice we received was this: *'If you're not turning down at least 20 per cent of meetings, you're not managing your time properly.'* If you've ever felt that at least one in five of the people at most of your meetings has no reason to be there, well, you're right.

For most employees, time wasted in meetings is a source of enormous frustration. There is however a very simple solution: just say no.

Before you agree to a meeting, ask yourself the following question: 'if I were sick, would this meeting be rescheduled?' If the answer is no, then you're not likely to have enough of an impact to make it worth your while. You'll waste your time and that of others. Decline the invitation by politely explaining that you don't think you would bring much to the table, but that you'd like a copy of the minutes. Then, enjoy the sweet taste of freedom.

According to a leading entrepreneur, another good way of turning down a meeting is to propose a three-minute one-on-one in its place. Apparently, this works 95 per cent of the time.

MAKE THE MOST OF YOUR TO-DO LIST

Bluma Zeigarnik was an early-twentieth-century Russian psychologist. One afternoon, while seated on the terrace of a busy Viennese café, she observed something peculiar. As the waiters rushed around, they seemed to have a remarkable grasp of the orders in progress while appearing to have instantly forgotten those already served. She hypothesized that we have a better memory of active tasks than of completed ones, and returned to her laboratory to put her theory to the test.

Bluma asked a group of children to complete 20 short activities involving puzzles, modeling clay, and so on. At the end of the day, when she asked the children to recall each activity, they remembered twice as many of the tests they hadn't fully completed as the ones they had. Today, we call this the Zeigarnik Effect, which, in a nutshell, states that an unfinished task takes up a lot more space in the brain than a completed one does.

You experience this all the time in your day-to-day life. A jumbled mental list of to-dos clouds your mind and prevents you from concentrating. Think of the brain as a computer hard drive: if you do too much at the same time, it's likely to overheat and slow down. For this reason, it's crucial to disentangle yourself from this 'black cloud' of interfering thoughts that serve only to weigh on your mind.

The best solution is to store everything on a kind of external hard-drive: your to-do list. You know all about to-do lists, of course, but in 95 per cent of cases, you're probably not using them to their full potential. The fact is, you should be using them obsessively. The moment you agree to do something, write it down, no questions asked. Same goes for good ideas. As soon as you have one, no matter where you are, write it down. Whether that's on a computer, a smartphone, a Post-it Note, or on a piece of paper, doesn't matter – just do it.

Systematically noting down each task on a to-do list frees up the mind. The last thing you want is to wake up in the middle of the night, your mind racing, having suddenly remembered you need to reply to the head of HR. Treat your to-do like you would a grocery list, adding to it each time you remember something you need rather than trying to remember everything all at once. It's the same principle.

Writing out each task also increases the likelihood of actually getting it done. The process of writing something down forces us to engage with it directly and sets us on the path towards completing it. A study was carried out on two similar groups, where those in the first group were asked to simply think about their goals and those in the second were asked to write them down. The findings showed that the people in the second group achieved on average 40 per cent more of their goals than did the first.

Take the time to describe each task you need to complete as precisely as possible. It may seem obvious, but as soon as the context in which you noted your tasks down changes, what once seemed clear may no longer make any sense at all.

Here's the format we suggest: an action verb followed by all the necessary information. For example, 'pick up the graphic layouts from Flora', 'write up the technical specifications for the emoji game', or 'write ten proposals for the title of a book on productivity'.

You could also try to frame your tasks around the result, i.e. instead of 'repair the broken window', try 'the window is repaired'. Focusing on the result is motivating; we prefer the idea of having a fixed window than the actual act of fixing it. Either method is good; what's most important is finding the one that best suits you, and sticking to it.

What you need

If you don't know where to start, here's a list of the tools most commonly used for a to-do list:

> A piece of paper. Obvious, but it'll do the job just fine. Unless you lose it.
> The basic note-taking tool that comes with your Mac or PC, such as TextEdit or Notepad. Already a step-up from the analog world of paper :)
> More technical note-taking apps. Entrepreneurs we spoke with also use <u>Google Keep</u>, <u>Notion</u>, <u>Any.do</u>, <u>Trello</u>, <u>Todoist</u>, and <u>Remember the Milk</u>. The main advantage of these apps is the ability to easily synchronize notes across different platforms, find what you need quickly, share documents easily, and filter by category.
> Voice activated search engines such as Siri or Google Voice can also be useful if you've got your hands full. If you're playing basketball for example, and you suddenly remember an important phone call, you can say out loud, 'Siri, remind me to call so-and-so when I get back to the office', and it'll happen. (Remember that both Siri and Google Voice let you create location-based reminders!)

The main thing here is to choose a tool you like and stick with it. Don't spend hours looking for the perfect app. What matters is how you use it.

THE TWO-MINUTE RULE

David Allen, author of the bestselling *Getting Things Done* came up with a simple yet powerful strategy he calls the Two-Minute Rule. Given the number of entrepreneurs that brought it up during our research, it's well worth looking into.

It's simple: if a task on your to-do list will take you less than two minutes to complete, do it. Immediately. You'll save yourself the time you'd have wasted re-reading it throughout the day or trying to squeeze it somewhere else into your schedule.

You might be surprised to find that most of our daily tasks actually take less than two minutes to complete. By doing these tasks straight away, we can dramatically reduce the number of items on our list and escape the psychological burden of an endless to-do.

DELEGATE, DELEGATE, DELEGATE

'If I want something done well, I'll do it myself.'
'This will get done quicker if I do it myself.'

'This is a no-brainer task – I'll set an example by handling it myself.'

Any of the above sound familiar? Then you aren't delegating enough. There is no task that only one person in the world is capable of doing: you can always delegate a task to someone else provided you invest enough time and energy in training them. Every time you look over your to-do list, the first thing you should ask yourself is, 'what can I delegate here?'.

Delegating isn't as straightforward as, say, forwarding an email. Initially, getting other people to do things in your place will take more time than if you just did them yourself as you'll have to invest time in training them. Yes, you'll lose time in the short-term – but again, you're investing time now in order to gain it back (and more) later on. Trust us, the return is worth it.

We were told countless times that the real secret to increasing productivity lies not in the work we do, but in the way we lead others. If you're a manager, the first thing you should be thinking about when you set foot in the office is not your personal tasklist, but that of your team. The quicker you can get them going at the start of the day, the faster you'll achieve your objectives.

How to delegate effectively

The purpose of this book is not to give you a lesson in management, but here are some of the main principles to bear in mind when delegating responsibility. Let's take a basic example.

You ask your intern to book a table at a restaurant for lunch with a client.

1. Communicate the purpose of the task. Explain the importance of the prospective contract to you and to the business.
2. Provide them with all the relevant information and as much context as you can. Give them the address of your client's office and an idea of the sort of restaurant they might like.
3. Give them a clear deadline. Explain that you need to give your client the address the day before the lunch at the latest so they can get organized.
4. Train them. Give them a list of websites to help them find the right restaurant. Invest the time now, so you won't have to next time.
5. Thank them. Whether you say it to their face, or write it down, it's important to acknowledge their effort (and it only takes a few seconds). If they didn't do a good job, provide them with feedback so next time they'll do better.

6. Finally, remember that when you delegate a task, it's the *end result* you're delegating. How they arrive there is not your concern (in other words, don't micromanage). If you don't have total confidence in your appointee, schedule regular check-ins with them so they don't go too far off-track.

Aside from coworkers, you might also consider delegating tasks to independent workers – that is, freelancers. They're a particularly great resource for entrepreneurs who typically have to take care of a lot of things they're not equipped to handle themselves, such as:

> Creating a visual identity and logo
> Building a website
> Writing content to attract visitors to your website
> Targeting potential clients

Don't spend months learning how to use Photoshop or Wordpress. Let the professionals do their jobs!

> Create a visual identity and logo => Freelance graphic designer
> Build a website => Freelance web developer
> Create content for your website => Freelance copywriter

> Target potential clients => Freelance lead genera-
> tion specialist

Finding the right freelancer is easier than you might think. You'll find a wealth of competent freelancers via platforms like Upwork which, at the time of writing, counts over ten million members.

A cheaper option is to go through sites such as Fiverr. They boast access to freelancers across the world who'll design your logo or create your website at a negligible cost (and with prices starting at $5, we really mean negligible). Of course, that price is not likely to get you much more than basic templates with little in the way of customization, but in some cases, that's all you need.

Another option for outsourcing repetitive tasks that aren't automatable is via the very well-known (and much-criticized) Amazon Mechanical Turk, which gives you access to hundreds of thousands of workers around the world capable of carrying out mechanical tasks. Up to you if you want to go there.

PRIORITIZE

Every minute you spend prioritizing your time is worth ten minutes of work time. Prioritizing your tasks is one of the most productive activities you can do in your day.

The Rule of 3

Imagine you have a big, empty jar in front of you. Beside it, there is a pile of rocks, a pile of pebbles and a pile of sand. Your job is to fit as much into the jar as you can.

Which order do you put them in?

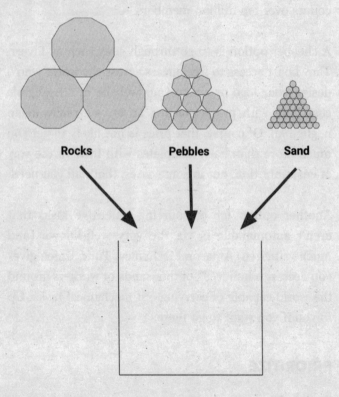

Rocks   Pebbles   Sand

If you work from smallest to largest, starting with a layer of sand, followed by the pebbles, there won't be enough space left for the rocks. If you start with the rocks, however, the pebbles will fit into the gaps in between while the sand will fill up any remaining space.

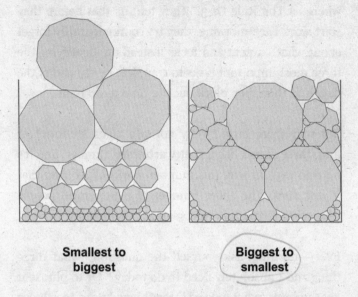

Smallest to biggest

Biggest to smallest

In his bestselling book *The 7 Habits of Highly Effective People*, Stephen Covey uses this metaphor to illustrate the way we tend to structure our work day. The jar represents your day, and the rocks, pebbles and sand are the jobs you need to get done. The rocks represent the most important tasks, the pebbles your secondary priorities, and the grains of sand all those small, little to-dos that don't provide much value. What Covey is saying is that if we concentrate first on the little tasks, there won't be enough space left in the day to take care of the big ones. So our first priority on any given day is to figure out what our big rocks are, and begin with those.

This was by and large *the* most widely-cited tip we received from the entrepreneurs we spoke to, and is known elsewhere as The Rule Of 3.[7] They told us that before they start work each morning, they try to momentarily forget about what's urgent and focus instead on identifying the three most important tasks to complete by the end of the day. And then they block out the time to do them.

But why three tasks? Why not two tasks, or four? At first, three seems like a pretty arbitrary number, and it's hard to explain why this number works other than that *it just does*. The sheer number of experienced people who seem to use this rule suggests the balance is right.

Every morning, ask yourself the question, 'what three things do I absolutely need to do today?' Or to phrase it another way, 'what are the three things I need to achieve to feel satisfied with my day's work?'

This tip goes hand in hand with another: always start with the hardest task. Take advantage of the fact that you tend to have the most energy first thing in the morning and get the hardest job out of the way first. If you start your day sorting emails and reading newsletters, you're liable to procrastinate – and you'll be forced to make up for it later in the day. If you can get the key

---

[7] The Rule of 3 originally comes from J.D. Meier's fantastic book on agile time management: *Getting Results the Agile Way* (2010).

tasks finished first, the rest of your day will fall into place. Mark Twain once said: 'Eat a live frog first thing in the morning and nothing worse will happen to you the rest of the day.' We agree.

Timeboxing

Once you've identified your three key tasks, you need to timebox them, which basically means blocking out whatever amount of time is necessary to get them done. Think of it as scheduling a meeting with yourself. Physically blocking out space in your schedule like this helps you avoid getting sidetracked by meetings and provides you with a dedicated time slot in which you can get the job done once and for all. If you follow the Rule of 3, you'll have around two or three timeboxed slots every day, which will automatically leave less space for meetings. With your day made up of timeboxes and only the most worthwhile meetings, your energy levels will stay high throughout the day. If you're extra-worried about getting looped into a bunch of meetings that may clog up your schedule, it's worth creating timeboxes in advance even if you don't know exactly what you'll be doing. Some of the entrepreneurs we spoke to simply label these 'work time' or else 'do not schedule anything'.

Most entrepreneurs suggested blocking out slots of one to two hours, but feel free to choose your own length of time. For example, you might try the Pomodoro method, which was invented by Francesco Cirillo, an Italian researcher who discovered that the optimum concentration period for the human brain is 25 minutes. He suggests breaking your schedule into 25-minute work periods punctuated by five-minute breaks. He named it after those kitchen timers in the form of a tomato (for a researcher, the man certainly has a good sense of marketing). You can of course choose longer work periods: to write this book we worked for two hours at a time with ten-minute breaks in-between (and that worked out pretty well for us).

It's important to remember that however long your time-boxes, your schedule is central to how you structure your work. So many of us tend to fill our schedules with nothing but meetings, be they with clients or coworkers – which is a shame. If you don't determine your own schedule, someone else will. By planning your day in a way that suits you, you'll be better organized to take on your key tasks and will avoid having your time hijacked by colleagues, emails, and newsletters. Make use of your calendar to plan your schedule and book time for important tasks.

Here are two types of calendars. Which one sounds like yours?

> A calendar that works: three clearly-timeboxed tasks, a few short meetings, time allocated for emails in three different slots spaced out across the day with a real break for lunch.

> A calendar that sucks: nothing timeboxed, too many long meetings, deadline reminders needlessly piling on pressure (there's no need to write down deadlines if you've allocated enough timeboxes to finish things off), and a quick, sad lunch at your desk.

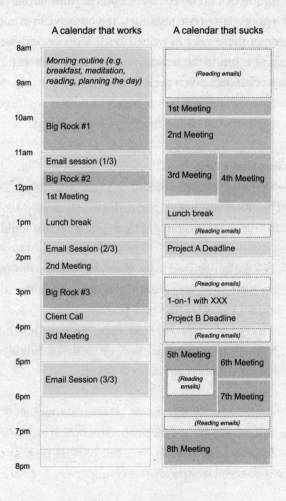

Offline time

Time spent in offline mode (when you're on a plane for example) represents a great opportunity to make some headway on your most important tasks. Many entrepreneurs told us that they take advantage of being cut off from emails, text messages, and other distractions to work on the tasks that require the most attention. If you need to work on reports or presentations using Google Docs or Slides, turn on offline access in the settings menu on Google Drive (drive. google.com) before you go: it'll take you five seconds, tops. Alternatively, if you've got a bunch of emails you need to write, activate the offline mode in Gmail settings.

Passive tasks first ✓

When we say 'passive tasks' we don't mean tasks you don't need to do at all, but rather tasks which simply require you to take one action to get them going. These could be:

> Delegation-related tasks such as briefing a coworker on a pitch or providing them with the material required to get started on a presentation.
> 'First-step' tasks such as requesting authorization from an administrative service, downloading a large file, or simply turning on the oven.

If you're faced with the choice between starting an active task or a passive one, go for the passive option first. Having set the process in motion, you can parallel process your active tasks while the passive task is underway. For example, if you're unsure whether to brief a graphic designer (a passive task), or crack on with a presentation (active task), brief the graphic designer first. That way, they can get on with the project while you simultaneously work on your presentation. Should you post a job ad first (passive task) or get going on an in-depth report (active task)? Take care of the job ad first: interested parties can get on with their applications, and you can write your report.

It works the same way in a kitchen. It'll take you twice as long to cook a dish if you work on each aspect of a recipe in sequence rather than starting with the passive tasks.

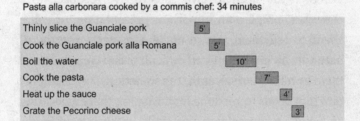

Pasta alla carbonara cooked by a commis chef: 34 minutes

Thinly slice the Guanciale pork	5'
Cook the Guanciale pork alla Romana	5'
Boil the water	10'
Cook the pasta	7'
Heat up the sauce	4'
Grate the Pecorino cheese	3'

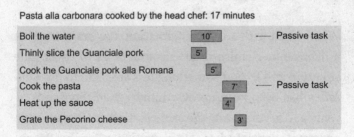

Pasta alla carbonara cooked by the head chef: 17 minutes

Boil the water	10'	—— Passive task
Thinly slice the Guanciale pork	5'	
Cook the Guanciale pork alla Romana	5'	
Cook the pasta	7'	—— Passive task
Heat up the sauce	4'	
Grate the Pecorino cheese	3'	

Seem like a no-brainer? It's not. In truth, confronted with the reality of a given working day, it's hard to resist diving into your to-dos, eyes closed. Your inclination will always be to jump in straight away, taking on tasks as they come. Instead, you should take the time to strategically identify passive tasks on your list and then get the ball rolling on those. They can be worked on in the background while you concentrate on the more important things.

FIGHT PROCRASTINATION

The last major hurdle on the road to productivity: procrastination.

Whether you need to give constructive feedback to a coworker, prepare an important presentation, or call a client to tell them you've made a mistake, we are all naturally inclined to put off difficult tasks. We get around them by telling ourselves there's something just as important that needs to get done first, whether that's answering an email, re-organizing our desk, or seeing what our friends are doing on Facebook.

When faced with a difficult situation, the brain triggers a defence mechanism that encourages us to resist that situation and to find something less stressful to do. This reflex has been built up over hundreds of thousands of years and is essentially the same instinct for survival our ancestors developed to avoid getting eaten by Saber-toothed tigers and to eat more sweet fruit.

This phenomenon is known as Laborit's Law, named after a French neurologist who researched man's tendency to avoid difficult situations and seek out pleasurable ones instead. When we experience something pleasant – such as drinking a sugary fruit juice, enjoying a pistachio ice cream or receiving a 'like' on one of our Instagram photos – the brain rewards us by releasing dopamine, a pleasure-generating chemical. In order to get more of this rewarding hormone, the brain prioritizes actions that reward us with immediate gratification over ones that take longer to complete.

Over the long term, procrastination can poison our lives, because the most important tasks – the ones that really test us, and will benefit us most in our personal and professional development – are invariably the most difficult.

Procrastination also has hidden consequences (or 'procrastination penalties') that don't always seem obvious:

> Financial Penalties: The longer you wait to book your flight, the more expensive the tickets will be. If you're late paying your bills, you'll have to pay a fine.
> Quality Penalties: If you don't give yourself enough time to get your project done properly, you risk compromising the end result. The same goes if you're commissioning a freelancer. The less time you give

them to complete a project, the more likely you are to end up with substandard work.

> Time Penalties: Leaving things to the last minute brings with it the risk of problems snowballing out of control. For example, if you leave your Christmas shopping till the last minute, you'll end up at the shops on 24 December queuing for hours. The same is true if you wait to book an appointment with your doctor, or a meeting with coworkers. The longer you put it off, the more likely it is that they'll already be booked.

Read on to learn about the best ways to stop procrastinating.

For complicated tasks, use the Ladder Technique

Let's take the example of a task that may seem daunting: writing a book. The size of the task makes it immediately discouraging, like trying to climb an impossibly high wall.

Writing
The Extra Hour

To overcome this, divide the project into a series of motivating, (i.e. simple, easy-to-complete) subtasks. Don't forget that your brain is always looking for immediate gratification, so it's important to write all these subtasks down on your to-do list. Crossing them off as you get things done means you'll stay motivated throughout the project.

If we return to the wall metaphor, the best way to climb over it is to build yourself a ladder made up of these smaller subtasks. When we wrote this book for example, our ladder had eight steps:

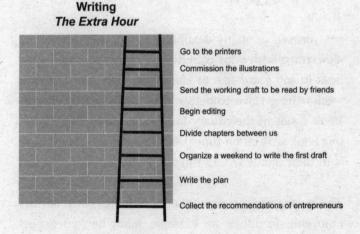

Writing
The Extra Hour

Go to the printers

Commission the illustrations

Send the working draft to be read by friends

Begin editing

Divide chapters between us

Organize a weekend to write the first draft

Write the plan

Collect the recommendations of entrepreneurs

The first step of the ladder could even be something that's seemingly unrelated to the project, but easy to achieve. As Admiral William McRaven, the officer who led the operation to catch Osama bin Laden in 2011 explained: 'if you make your bed every morning you will have accomplished the first task of the day. It will give you a small sense of pride and it will encourage you to do another task, and another ... ' If you don't do the small things, you'll never get the big things done.

For unpleasant tasks, just get started
a. Deadlines
One of the most obvious ways of avoiding procrastination is to set yourself a precise deadline. If you have to give a presentation at 9am, you don't have a choice, you panic, and then you get it done.

Set yourself as many deadlines as you can. Finding it slow going with your commercial strategy? Email your boss to say you'd like to show him your progress in a week's time. Have to deliver bad news to a coworker? Book a slot in their diary for the following day. To get our book written on time, we told everyone they'd have it in their hands within three months.

The entrepreneurs we spoke to also suggested setting enjoyable deadlines: for example, many booked a sport session for 7pm to prevent themselves from hanging around too late at the office. It's worth booking in a few workouts or after-work outings each week to stop you from spending too much time behind your desk.

b. The first second

We tend to think that we need to be motivated to make something happen. Turns out, it's the opposite: we need to make something happen to be motivated. If you want to motivate yourself to go for a run, jog 30 feet. If you want to motivate yourself to write, penning the first few words will alleviate empty-page anxiety. The novelist Stephen Pressfield writes: 'There's a secret that real writers know that wannabe writers don't, and the secret is this: it's not the writing part that's hard. What's hard is sitting down to write. What keeps us from sitting down is resistance.'

The first second is always the hardest, but once you've started, it'll be a lot easier.

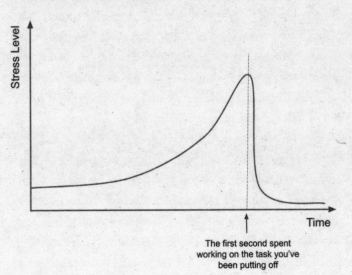

The first second spent working on the task you've been putting off

Got a difficult call to make? Start by picking up the phone and dialing the number. Have a tough email to write? Start with the first few words.

For boring tasks, organize Power Hours

Filling in a database, writing out an expense form, resizing photos ... If a job bores you, it's probably because it's repetitive and has limited added value. You need to find a way to make it more fun. Gather your coworkers, put on some music, and lay out some snacks. Some people refer to this a 'War Room' or 'Power Hours', and it's a great way to get things done. You could also turn the job into a challenge by looking for a way to automate it once and for all. We've dedicated a whole section to this subject in the 'Accelerate' chapter.

To-do list to 'Get organized':

Allocate enough time and energy to the projects that matter the most to you:

> Say no to all incoming requests that do not align with your priorities. This requires that you clearly define your objectives and that you keep them in mind at all times.

> Note down each task on your to-do list to free up your mind and eliminate your 'black cloud' of interfering thoughts. You will also maximize your odds of actually completing these tasks.

> If a task on your to-do list will take you less than two minutes to complete, just do it. Immediately. You'll save yourself the time you'd have wasted re-reading it throughout the day or trying to squeeze it somewhere else into your schedule.

> Invest time in training and coaching people around you and delegate as much as you can.

> Prioritize your day with the Rule of 3: what are the top three things that, once done, will make you happy at the end of the day?

> After you've identified these three tasks, timebox them. In other words, allocate a slot in your calendar for the time needed to complete them. Think of it as scheduling a meeting with yourself.

> When you scan your to do list, identify 'passive tasks' and start with them. Once you've initiated them, you will be able to complete other tasks in parallel and will get things done faster as a result.

> Understand what causes you to procrastinate and take the right actions accordingly. If a task is too complex, use the ladder technique by breaking it down into simple, easy-to-achieve subtasks. If the task is unpleasant, set yourself a deadline and remember that the first second is always the hardest, but once you've started, it'll be a lot easier. If the task seems boring, find a way to make it fun and enjoyable.

CHAPTER 2

CONCENTRATE

If you had started your professional career in the 1960s, your office would have looked quite different. You'd have your own desk with some fountain pens and a stack of files in one corner, an assistant to type out your letters, and every now and then your phone would ring.

Most noticeably, you'd have had significantly fewer distractions: in short, the complete opposite of today's work environment. Essentially this can be attributed to three phenomena:

1. The open-plan revolution: while the great open space of the modern workplace has certainly reduced costs and eased communication, it has also paved the way for a host of disruptions and interruptions.
2. The omnipresence of phones and computers: our devices have certainly helped us work faster, but they also encourage rapid switching between tasks (AKA multitasking). We can google search in one click, switch to our Facebook page, and then finish an Excel spreadsheet … The prevalence of computers and smartphones has also massively increased the number of messages we receive. In the past, letters were rare and required effort: you'd have to first write the letter, then buy a stamp, then mail it …

Today a message costs nothing and requires hardly any energy to write. As a result, we are bombarded with hundreds of them each day. Although useful in certain contexts, the practice of copying in (CCing) coworkers is also heavily overused, largely for political gain as in 'look how well I've been working', or 'I'm going to tell you about this so I don't need to take responsibility should there be a problem'.

3. The explosion in content providers: media and social networks have entered the era of infobesity. Eric Schmidt, Google's executive chairman from 2001 to 2017 estimated that in 2010, it took just three days to produce the same amount of information as in all of 2003. Concentration is becoming our rarest resource.

It's estimated that today, the average office employee works for only 11 minutes[8] between interruptions. Alternating between tasks gives the illusion of productivity: employees believe that they're working full-speed ahead, responding quickly to a multitude of demands.

The reality of course is quite different. Multitasking is one of productivity's biggest enemies. This principle even has a name: Carlson's Law, after the Swedish researcher who theorized back in the 1950s that it takes significantly less time and energy to complete a task in one go than

---

[8] Gloria Mark, University of California, Irvine.

it does if you continuously stop and start. To put it another way, it's much more efficient to do A and then B than to do both at the same time. It takes a lot of time to get your concentration back 100 per cent when you shift attention from one thing to the next: each time you're interrupted, you have to recover your initial degree of focus – much like being woken from a deep sleep.

A job started should always be finished before moving on to the next. Remember the ladder analogy we used earlier? Once you've made it up that first step, you're ready to climb all the rest. If you kept switching rungs, up then down, you'd lose all your momentum.

Alternating between tasks doesn't just slow you down, it also diminishes your intellectual capacity. Professor and psychologist Glenn Wilson led a study that showed we risk losing the equivalent of ten IQ points if we are interrupted while solving a problem. That interruption could be something as seemingly benign as receiving an email.

The most productive people are those who are 100 per cent focused on what they are doing at a given moment. In a meeting, they put all their energy into driving the relevant topic forward, solving problems, and making positive steps. In a training session, they are concentrated on absorbing all the information they can. When they work, they give their full concentration to the task at hand and don't check their emails or Facebook pages every five minutes.

The purpose of this chapter is to give you the tools you need to avoid those distractions and interruptions and to stay 100 per cent focused on whatever you're doing.

Why interruptions are costly

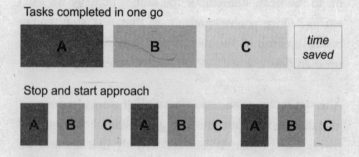

Tasks completed in one go

Stop and start approach

ELIMINATE INTERFERING THOUGHTS

The main threat to concentration is that 'black cloud' of interfering thoughts we mentioned earlier on in this book. Mind-polluting thoughts tend to fall into the same category. They're the things you mustn't forget to do: wrap up this report, reply to so-and-so, get in touch with a supplier, or simply go and pick up your shirt from the dry cleaners.

The first technique you should rely on to avoid these distractions is the to-do list that we detailed in the previous chapter. As soon as a new to-do pops into your mind, write it down without worrying too much about the specifics or how much time it's going to take. Then put it to one side, knowing that it's safely stored in your much more reliable external memory. We're lucky that in today's world, we've always got something to note things down on: the second a task springs to mind, you can just whip out your smartphone and type it into whatever to-do list app you prefer.

Read on to learn about three additional tips and tools to help you concentrate.

Boomerangs

Having to remember to chase up clients or coworkers can cause enormous stress. Luckily, there are some good email tools on the market to make your life easier. Mixmax is an add-on for Gmail that reminds you to follow up on an email if you haven't received a reply within a set timeframe. An equivalent tool for Outlook is Boomerang. Simply install the add-on and if you don't hear back in the time you've specified, these tools will ping you to follow up. One more load off your mind. You can even pre-write an email to be sent automatically after a set number of days. To do this, click on 'send later' and type in the date and time of your choice. Mixmax will even suggest the best time to send your email to increase the likelihood of a quick response. If you're sending a quote to a client for example, it's better to send it at a time when they're available to get back to you immediately. Another example: you could schedule a rejection email to an unsuccessful job interviewee to be sent the following day – far kinder than sending it the moment they leave the room.

Inbox Zero

Inbox Zero is a classic method for increasing productivity and is used by over a third of the entrepreneurs we met with. The premise is simple: keeping your inbox empty keeps your mind calm. Think of your inbox like your mailbox at home: when you pick up your mail, you don't leave a few letters for next time – so why treat your inbox any differently? The best way to achieve this is by archiving your emails. That way, they stay invisible while remaining accessible via the search bar. Think of them like items in a backpack: invisible to the outside, but readily available when you need them.

The Inbox Zero Method in three stages:

> As soon as you read an email that doesn't require an action, archive it straight away.
> If an action on your part is needed and you have time, reply and then archive the email.[9]
> If you don't have time, add the action required to your to-do list and then archive the email. Remember that you should have only one centralized to-do list to prioritize tasks effectively.

The only real risk you face with Inbox Zero is that you could actually end up wasting time by obsessively trying to keep your inbox empty. This is in fact entirely counter-productive. Incessantly clearing away emails ends up

---

[9] Enabling the 'Send and Archive' button in the Gmail Settings menu will bring up a button you can use to automatically archive a conversation once you've sent your reply.

The Inbox Zero method

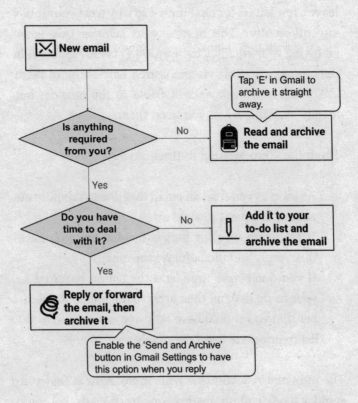

New email

Is anything required from you?

No → **Read and archive the email**

Tap 'E' in Gmail to archive it straight away.

Yes ↓

Do you have time to deal with it?

No → **Add it to your to-do list and archive the email**

Yes ↓

Reply or forward the email, then archive it

Enable the 'Send and Archive' button in Gmail Settings to have this option when you reply

becoming a distraction in itself, taking your focus away from the real priorities. What's important here is getting your work done, not having an empty inbox. An appropriate approach would be to aim for Inbox Zero twice a week – Wednesdays and Fridays, for example. In the same way that you leave the office with some work unfinished at the end of the day, you can accept leaving a few of your emails unread.

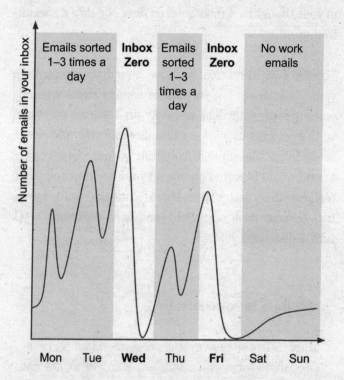

A clean desk

The first thing you see at work is your desk. The objects that clutter up your desk are more often than not the things that still need to be finished: a file you need to read, a contract you need to sign, a letter that needs to be mailed, etc. Positioned on your desk, they serve as distracting reminders that steer your mind away from the task at hand. A disorganized desk is like an unavoidable to-do list right in front of your eyes – and therefore in your thoughts. A disorganized desk equals a disorganized mind.

To keep your mind clear and free from distractions, keep your desk clean. Put in place a weekly ritual whereby you organize your desk properly on a Friday afternoon so that you get to work on Monday morning and you're ready to go. The same rule applies to your virtual office: get rid of old files that clutter up your desktop and you'll feel incredibly better (Hazel for Mac automatically moves files on your desktop that haven't been used for a week into a dedicated folder).

Meditate to concentrate

More than one in five entrepreneurs regularly practices some form of meditation. Many of us are apt to write off meditation as something for either Buddhist monks or lost hippies, and yet meditation (or the art of doing nothing) is now embraced by millions of people the world over – including successful businessmen and women. Why?

In part due to the work of Soren Gordhamer, who having divorced, lost his job and become addicted to Twitter, decided to disappear and go live in a mobile home in a remote part of New Mexico. In search of a way to change his life, he spent his days studying key meditation texts, eventually recognizing that in a world dominated by innumerable digital disruptions, practising meditation can teach us to regain our focus, improving our ability to concentrate and in turn, improving the quality of our work.

Soon afterwards, Gordhamer wrote a book lauding the virtues of meditation that quickly became popular within Silicon Valley's high-tech, results-based culture. On the back of the book's success, he set up the Wisdom 2.0 Conference which quickly earned cult status among the industry's many entrepreneurs. Each year, the conference brings together leaders from the world's biggest tech companies, including the founders of Facebook, Twitter, LinkedIn, and Paypal. All these companies run hugely successful programs based on Gordhamer's ideas.

Contrary to popular belief, meditation is not about emptying the mind, but rather embracing the thoughts that come into our heads, acknowledging them for what they are, and then refocusing on ourselves and our meditation practice. Although mental training is not its original purpose, it turns out meditation is a fantastic method for improving our ability to concentrate.

Of course, to see its real benefits, a disciplined approach is crucial. If you are interested in trying it out, we recommend finding a week-long intensive course. There are various approaches, but *Vipassana* was recommended to us many, many times. An alternative would be to download an app for your smartphone, such as Headspace, Calm, or Insight Timer (the top-rated free meditation app developed by teachers the world over). Even if you only meditate for ten minutes a day, you'll quickly notice the benefits.

SHIELD YOURSELF FROM TEMPTATION

Most social networks and media outlets were constructed with one main objective: to hold on to your attention for as long as possible. Why? The longer you spend on their platform, the more money they make.

Sites like Netflix and YouTube know that it's harder to press 'stop' than 'play next', which is why they invented auto-play. News sites increasingly use clickbaity ads, because they know your curiosity can't resist. Facebook and Instagram try to incite you to use their platforms by notifying you of new likes by any means necessary. There's a physiological reason that explains why we can't resist these distractions: the brain responds to the satisfaction of short-term desire by releasing a thrilling shot of dopamine (that same pleasure-giving hormone that encourages us to procrastinate).

So the best solution is to protect yourself from ... yourself. If you find it impossible not to polish off that pot of Nutella, the best way to avoid doing so is to not buy it in the first place. The same principle applies to tempting work distractions: cut off access at the source. For this, there are two types of tools at your disposal:

1. **Blocking apps**. There are various apps available (such as Freedom) which you can set up to block your access to particular websites or apps for a specific amount of time. Also, on your smartphone, try moving all your social network apps such as Facebook and Instagram to the second or third screen, or better yet, uninstall them completely. You'll still be able to access them via your phone's web browser if you need to. It's slightly disconcerting at first, but after four or five days you'll feel a newfound sense of freedom. Finally, if you're meeting someone for a

coffee, don't leave your phone on the table. That way you'll be less tempted to check it and you'll make the person you're with feel that they count more than the next 'like' that pops up on your screen.

2. **Bookmarking/Parking apps.** Our first instinct when someone sends us a video or article is to open it immediately. To avoid the temptation, it's important to have an efficient way of filing them away for later. We recommend Pocket, an excellent extension for Chrome, that lets you save articles and videos with one click, which you can pull up later on any device.

Of course, be honest with yourself: if you really can't resist the call of social media, take a 15-minute break, do what you need to, and then get back to your work without distractions.

CREATE A BUBBLE

We're not saying you need to live like a hermit or avoid your coworkers at all costs, but if you really need to get something done, it's important to be able to shut yourself off from distractions. And for that, many entrepreneurs make use of a formidable weapon:

Headphones.

Two reasons wearing headphones is so effective:

1. It demonstrates to your colleagues that you're working on something important and don't want to be disturbed.

2. Listening to music can help us concentrate. But not just any music – you'll want to listen to something easy-going that doesn't require too much attention. Simple music, preferably without lyrics (think classical, relaxed jazz, or a nice film soundtrack as opposed to Britney Spears or Adele). Try and avoid new releases even if it means listening to your favorite playlist on repeat: the brain is less distracted by familiar songs than by new ones.[10] It's also worth trying out the excellent website (and Google Chrome extension) Noisli. It provides dozens of background soundscapes that can help you concentrate, from quiet riverbanks, to cafés, to a cabin during a thunderstorm. Ambient sound can really help create an atmosphere that's conducive to work. According to a study from the University of Chicago, a light distraction in your ambient environment actually benefits the creative process. That's no doubt why you have your best ideas while showering, brushing your teeth or mowing the lawn …

---

[10] Morgan K. Ward & Joseph K. Goodman & Julie R. Irwin, 'The same old song: The power of familiarity in music choice.' *Marketing Letters*, 25 (2014): 1–11.

That said, there is an option that's even better than putting on headphones: get away from the office. Try working in a café, a park, a co-working space, wherever you want. Spending time away from the distractions of the office allows you to really concentrate on the things you need to. The entrepreneurs we met considered time away from their desks a crucial part of the week, and some of them even block out one morning each week just for that purpose. You'd be amazed at how much you can achieve with half a day of uninterrupted work.

An even more radical approach: go isolate yourself somewhere far away for a few days and work on whatever you need to. Twice a year, Bill Gates heads off to a remote cabin on the Canadian border for a 'Think Week' without anyone (not even friends or family). Entirely alone, he spends his time reading and reflecting on his life objectives and the future of his business. He claims that the ideas that paved the way for Microsoft's most groundbreaking innovations came to him during these 'Think Weeks'.

Several entrepreneurs told us they experience a state of intense psychological satisfaction during periods of hyper-concentration when cut off from the outside world. The psychologist Mihály Csíkszentmihályi famously refers to this state as 'flow'. When we are entirely focused on a task, not only do we become extremely effective, but we also gain a sensation of intense joy, a kind of ecstasy in which we seem to lose all concept of time. You may have already experienced this flow state when playing the piano, climbing mountains, or even writing. So why can't we attain it through our work?

But what if you're thinking: 'My boss will NEVER let me work outside the office'? Approach the problem by asking them to let you try just once. That day, work as hard as you can and send them an email detailing everything you've achieved. We're willing to bet they'll leave you to it. Generally, your boss's open-mindedness when it comes to working outside the office is directly related to the quality of the work you produce.

Dealing with time wasters

So, you've tried hard to create your bubble ... some of your coworkers leave you to it, but some keep coming to you for an opinion or an approval. Then there are the chatterboxes who simply won't stop talking and who, just when you think they've finished, veer off onto some other unrelated topic.

These people are time wasters. Nice in short doses, but incredibly annoying after a while. Here's our advice on getting them to stop bothering you.

1. For the people who won't stop interrupting you, it's straightforward: tell them you need all your concentration to finish whatever it is you're do-ing and tell them to come back at a specific time (and for a specific duration) with a precise list of questions. The time spent thinking out their questions will usually be enough for them to work out the majority of the answers themselves.

2. Dealing with chatterboxes is a little more com-plicated. Chatterboxes crave your attention, so you need to find a way of breaking their flow of words and making them understand that you need to get back to your work. Try slowly rais-ing your hand as though to say stop, responding briefly to whatever it was they were talking about and explaining why you have to get back to your work, e.g. 'I have a presentation I need to finish by 3pm so I really need to get back to it straight away.' And, remember to keep your cool:)

CHOOSE ASYNCHRONOUS COMMUNICATION

Allow us to introduce you to two somewhat pedantic-sounding terms: synchronous and asynchronous commu-nication. One of them equals trouble.

1. Synchronous communication: this is when both parties communicate at the same time, as in face-to-face and phone conversations.
2. Asynchronous communication: this is when neither party is required to respond immediately, as in letters, emails or text messages.

Of course, the boundary between the two isn't always so clearly-defined. For example, a phone conversation becomes asynchronous if you leave a voicemail, and you could argue that responding immediately to an email makes it synchronous rather than asynchronous.

The key point is that synchronous communication threatens your productivity because it requires your immediate involvement and therefore interrupts your work. We are not suggesting you should abandon your phone entirely, but you might want to try limiting its use to either:

1. Situations that are too complicated to be dealt with via email. According to *The 3 Email Rule* by Phil Simon, if you need to send more than three emails to someone on one subject, you should be talking. Ideally, plan your call with the other party in advance to avoid causing unnecessary interruption.
2. Real emergencies. For example: your website goes down, there's a breakdown in the production line, or your most important client needs a quick answer.

In all other cases, prioritize asynchronous communication.

Forget the phone

Several entrepreneurs we spoke to told us they tend to not answer the phone if they don't recognize the caller, and many take it a step further by not answering the phone at all. This makes sense in a way: most of the time, the person making the call is doing so because it's convenient for them, though this is rarely the case for the person on the receiving end of that call. You could argue that people who call you are in essence, stealing your time. You probably should pick up if it's your boss or an important client calling, but draw the line there. Some of the people we spoke to suggested leaving a voicemail encouraging callers to send a text rather than leave a message, as in: 'Hi, you've reached Paul. I don't listen to my voicemail, but send me a text and I'll get back to you as quickly as I can.' If your job allows, we strongly encourage you to do the same thing. Otherwise, there's always the nuclear option: deactivate voicemail completely (the process will vary depending on your carrier, but you'll find what you need with a quick google search).

Don't check your emails more than three times per day

The average employee checks their emails once every fifteen minutes. You don't mind waiting three or four hours for someone to get back to your emails, right? Give yourself permission to do the same, and limit the number of times you check your inbox to two or three per day to avoid needless interruption (for example at 10am, 2pm and 6pm). Think of it like doing laundry: you don't wash dirty clothes individually; you wait until you've got a full load. Citing Tim Ferriss, author of *The 4-Hour Workweek*, one entrepreneur suggested setting up an auto-reply explaining that you only check your emails at such and such time each day, and to send a text message if it's really important.

To help you resist the temptation to check emails as they arrive, we recommend using Gmail's 'Inbox when Ready' extension, which hides your inbox by default. The result: you get to write emails and get on with your work without being disturbed each time a new message arrives. The only way you can view your inbox is by clicking on 'Show Inbox'. By letting you take back control, Inbox when Ready has become one of Gmail's highest-rated extensions, and with good reason. The equivalent for PC is Boomerang and its Inbox Pause feature.

Above all, do not, we repeat, *do not* read work emails outside of office hours. Remember the Zeigarnik Effect we mentioned earlier: if you read a work email on a Sunday when you're unable to do whatever is required straight away, you are feeding that black cloud of intrusive thoughts with unfinished mental to-dos. The only prize you get is two hours of needless stress in the middle of the weekend. Leave your emails for Monday morning. If your colleagues want to work weekends, that's up to them – but let them know that you won't. And do unto others as you'd have them do unto you: if ever you do need to write an important email on your day off, put it on your weekday to-do or schedule it to be sent on Monday morning (we'll show you how in the 'Acceleration' chapter).

Email 1 – Chat 0

Despite what their creators may claim, chat apps like Slack or Microsoft Teams are not about to replace email. The fact that email allows you to communicate with anyone regardless of platform (Gmail, Yahoo, Outlook, etc.) means that it will remain the primary digital tool for outside communication. Although chat apps can certainly facilitate communication internally, the most important messages tend to get lost amid funny links and where-are-we-getting-lunch debates. We recommend using email for anything important and chat apps for the more light–hearted stuff. The added bonus here is that by systematically using emails, you'll have automatically filed anything important in the same place, making it easier to find in the future.

DISABLE NOTIFICATIONS

Alongside constant interruptions from those around us, we also have to deal with being interrupted by our devices. In 9 out of 10 cases, these notifications are unnecessary and serve only to prevent you from concentrating. Our advice:

1. Switch off almost all notifications on your smartphone and your computer (with the exception of things like flight info, taxi arrival alerts, etc.). Don't waste time adjusting the settings for each individual app, simply open up the preferences menu on your iPhone, Android, Mac, or Windows device and change the settings for all notifications and alerts at once. Takes a minute, but saves you hours.

2. Life's too short to waste time watching pre-roll ads or hunting for that little 'x' to close a pop-up window. Install an Adblocker such as Adblock in your browser (but consider turning it off on the websites you like – it's how they stay alive).

3. Unsubscribe from any newsletters you don't absolutely need. Here's a good rule of thumb: if ever you think, 'this may come in handy one day', unsubscribe. Only keep newsletters you can't do without. If you haven't read a newsletter's last five sendouts, odds are you'll never read any of them. Unsubscribe. It's the same for clothes you haven't worn in the past 12 months: give them away. There are websites you can use such as Unroll.me that are designed to save you the trouble of having to unsubscribe from each newsletter individually, but just know that they do harvest and sell your (anonymous) data too.

To-do list to 'Concentrate':

Alternating between tasks will slow you down; you need to avoid distractions and interruptions to stay 100 per cent focused.

> Eliminate interfering thoughts by using an 'external hard drive': your to-do list. Write down all your ideas, as soon as they go through your head.

> Use 'boomerangs', i.e. tools that will remember to automatically follow-up with people who have yet to reply to your emails.

> Try the 'Inbox Zero' methodology to gain peace of mind when it comes to managing your emails. To do this, archive all the emails that you have processed (they are invisible to you but still accessible if you search for them via the search bar).

> Set up a weekly routine to clean your (actual and virtual) desk. This will help keep your mind clear and free from distractions.

> Protect yourself from temptations by installing social network blocking tools or 'parking' tools to put content aside and make that content available for later.

> Put on headphones to signal to your colleagues that you are working on an important task and that you do not want to be disturbed.

> Work remotely at least half a day every week to be fully focused and get things done.

> With the exception of emergencies or problems that are complex to solve, use asynchronous communications, which allow people to reply when the time is appropriate for them (email, text message ...).

> Do not answer phone calls from numbers that you do not recognize.

> Limit the number of times you check your inbox to two or three per day to avoid needless interruption. And never read work emails on weekends if you want to avoid feeding that black cloud of intrusive thoughts with unfinished mental to-dos.

> Disable (almost) all notifications from your smartphone and your computer: it will take a minute, but it will save you hours of concentration. And unsubscribe from all promotional newsletters that you don't read.

CHAPTER 3

ACCELERATE

It's 7.30pm. You're alone in the kitchen surrounded by bags of groceries. An hour from now, you've got 15 friends coming over for dinner. Panic ensues.

You've got several options: you could *get organized* (by starting the passive tasks in your recipe, for example), or *concentrate* (i.e. switch off the TV), but chances are that neither of these will get that dinner cooked fast enough. What you need to do here is to *accelerate*. For this, try these four steps.

1.   Fundamentals: create a solid foundation for yourself that will help you save time on future tasks. In this case: take a long, deep breath, clear your worktop, and sharpen your knives.
2.   Automation: automate any repetitive action you can. In the case of your dinner party, you might ask to borrow your neighbor's blender and electric mixer.
3.   Speed: speed up manual tasks. For your dinner party, make use of some good knife techniques to peel and chop your vegetables as quickly as possible (if you don't know any knife techniques, start watching *Masterchef*).
4.   Twenty/Eighty Rule: forget 100 per cent. Settle for making an 80 per cent impact that requires a 20

per cent effort. In other words, forget the lightly-spiced Madagascan redcurrant sauce and go for homemade mayonnaise.

Fundamentals, **A**utomation, **S**peed, **T**wenty/Eighty Rule: welcome to the FAST method. If it works well in the kitchen, it does wonders at work.

How do you determine the actual value of an investment in your time?

Throughout this chapter, we've suggested several useful tools, some of which you have to pay for. To work out whether they're worth the cash, you first need to put a price on your time.

The following exercise will help you figure out how much an hour of your time is worth.

For some – consultants, for example – the answer is pretty straightforward, because they already charge their clients by the hour. Same goes for sales executives, who know than an hour of work can potentially bring in X amount of money. For those whose salaries aren't directly proportional to the time they've put in, it's a little more complex. The easiest solution is to make a calculation based on your salary. To get a rough idea of your hourly wage, divide your take-home monthly salary (that is, after taxes) by the number of hours you work each month.

For example, if each month you earn $6,000 and work 150 hours, your hourly rate is 6,000/150 = $40.

Knowing this will make it easier to decide whether investing in a certain tool or even outsourcing it entirely is worth it or not.

> If an app costs $35 but will save an hour of your time each month, tell your boss it's a worthwhile investment.
> If a $10 taxi will save you half an hour on your journey, jump in! Ultimately, it'll save the business money.

You should also think about adding a subjective value to the task. Whilst it's important to think of the economic costs, a daunting task also has a psychological cost that shouldn't be underestimated. Investing in an app that takes care of your expense reports will bring you peace of mind – an asset that transcends financial gain. Ultimately, the key thing here is to know how much money you're prepared to spend to save an hour of your time.

FUNDAMENTALS: GET THE CONDITIONS RIGHT FOR A GOOD START

'Give me six hours to chop down a tree and I'll spend the first four sharpening the axe.' This quote, attributed by some to Abraham Lincoln means to say that time spent preparing for something is just as important as the time spent carrying it out.

For example, experienced web developers working on complex projects will spend between 20 and 80 per cent of their time planning and formulating their ideas before they write a single line of code.

Before you start, sharpen your axe.

Relax

If you were off hiking in the mountains and you'd just exhausted yourself scaling a peak, your first instinct probably wouldn't be to keep going right away. You'd stop for a break, knowing intuitively that your body needed rest.

Unfortunately, we tend not to apply this same logic when it comes to the mind. We rush from one meeting to the next or dive head-first into an important presentation even though we're already exhausted. In the same way that we recognize the limits of our physical capacity, we should also acknowledge that our cognitive ability is not limitless. Concentration requires a huge amount of energy: the average adult brain uses between 20 and 25 per cent of the body's total energy consumption despite representing only 2 per cent of its weight.

Make sure you take enough breaks in your day – real ones. A break isn't just time spent not working or being lazy, it is a fundamental requirement for improving efficiency and creativity. Don't feel guilty about taking a real lunch break or about scheduling some downtime between meetings. If, midway through a task you feel your energy levels drop, stop and move on to something less demanding. You can always return to it later. One of the entrepreneurs we spoke to told us he draws a distinction between cerebral tasks that require deep focus – which he does at the start of the day – and jobs that don't, which he leaves until later.

If you're really wiped, do what Air Force pilots do and take a power nap. A 10 to 15-minute snooze will boost your energy levels and keep you going for another three or four hours.

It's no coincidence that history's greatest thinkers regularly alternated between working and relaxing. Charles Darwin divided his working day into just three 90-minute sessions; the rest of the time, he was out walking in the woods or reading (none of which stopped him from writing one of the most revolutionary books in the history of science). The mathematical genius Henri Poincaré worked in two stints, first from 10 to 12 in the morning and then from 5 to 7 in the afternoon. He dedicated the rest of his time to walking in the mountains and taking naps. Le Corbusier, the architect credited with inventing urbanism, only arrived at the office in the afternoon after spending the whole morning painting.

How the masters organized their days[11]

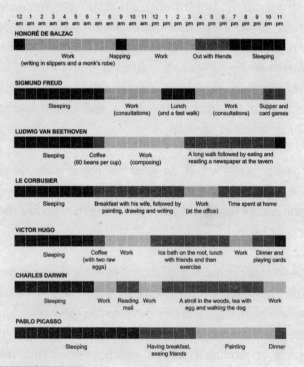

[11] Source: https://podio.com/site/creative-routines.

Decision fatigue: how to preserve your energy for important decisions

You're going to bed: do you set the alarm for 7 or 8am?

You get up in the morning: tea or coffee?

You're getting dressed: long or short sleeves?

You get to work: what do you check first, your emails or your calendar?

You go out for lunch with a client: which restaurant do you choose?

Each day we make hundreds of micro-decisions like these that take up both time and energy as we first define our options, weigh the pros and cons of each, and then make a choice. The end result is decision fatigue, a condition you may already be familiar with. The cumulative effect of all these micro-decisions is that we drain ourselves of the time and energy we need to make important decisions, like whether or not to hire a candidate, start a new project, etc. Certain researchers claim that we have a limited store of willpower that gets used up with each decision we make on a given day. They argue that as the day progresses and our willpower is exhausted, we are guided less by reason and more by what we perceive to be the easiest solution. It's worth noting that this theory is somewhat controversial and doesn't enjoy widespread support among the scientific community.

How far should you go to fight decision fatigue?

Some people go to great lengths to reduce the number of micro-decisions they make each day. An extreme example of this is Facebook founder Mark Zuckerberg, who only ever wears grey t-shirts in order to 'clear [his] life so that [he has] to make as few decisions as possible about anything except how to best serve [the Facebook] community'. It's the same reasoning behind Steve Jobs' black turtlenecks and Barack Obama's blue suits. Some people eat exactly the same breakfast each day and stick to a fixed set of meals each week in order to avoid unnecessary decisions.

In our humble opinions, if you're sacrificing your personal life for your professional one, then you're taking things too far. Our advice would be to learn to make decisions quickly by self-limiting your options. The speed with which society evolves is breathtaking: how do you choose a hotel from the hundreds online? How do you choose a breakfast cereal from an entire aisle of options? How do you choose a restaurant when three new ones open every day in your city? By limiting your own options, you keep your decisions straightforward. If you need to find a wine bar to meet at with friends, pick any three and force yourself to choose from those. Failing that, find a place and become a regular there: you'll make friends with the boss and might even score a few free drinks.

A healthy mind in a healthy body

Western culture tends to perceive body and mind as being entirely independent of one another: the mind commands and the body acts. Now, doctors and neuroscientists are discovering that this relationship is far more complex than previously imagined.

Exercise

Lots of our entrepreneurs endorsed morning runs or lunchtime workouts (running, yoga, CrossFit, squash …) as ways to up their concentration and productivity for the rest of the day. Others simply walk or bike to work to give their minds a rest and arrive at work energized and ready to start the day.

During exercise, the body releases all kinds of hormones into your system. There are endorphins, of course, which help make you feel good – but the biggest boost comes from dopamine, which reduces tiredness and increases your concentration and memory throughout the day. So in short, exercise requires energy, but it gives it back, with interest.

Stay in shape with a seven-minute workout

It all started with five paragraphs published in the *New York Times* in September 2013. The article described a study carried out by the American College of Sports Medicine concerning a new training method that, despite being just seven minutes long, promised similar results to prolonged endurance training. It created such a buzz that the *New York Times* went on to release a seven-minute workout app which has since been downloaded millions of times.

There are now around 30 similar apps on both the App Store and Google Play Store. If you ask us, the best one is Johnson & Johnson's 7 Minute Workout in which a virtual trainer named Chris takes you through the method one step at a time.

In a nutshell, the 7 Minute Workout consists of twelve 30-second exercises performed one after the other (push-ups, crunches, squats, planks) with a

10-second break between each one. You can do it anywhere you like: all you need is a chair and a wall.

If you want something where you can customize time and set goals, the Sworkit App was also highly recommended by the entrepreneurs we interviewed.

Diet

We tend to ascribe a lot of importance to 'gut feelings' – and contemporary research is starting to show us why.

The digestive system is more than just a series of organs designed to process food and transform it into fuel for the body. It's more like a second brain: our intestines contain over 200 million neurons – as many as in a dog's brain – and more nerve cells than our eyes, ears or skin.

Scientists discovered that electrically stimulating the vagus nerve (the nerve responsible for communication between the brain and the digestive system) could have dramatic effects on a subject's mood.

We're not going to preach about the virtues of carrots and sprouted grains, but it's worth bearing in mind that what you eat has a much bigger impact on your state of mind and energy levels than you may realize. Play around and see what works best for you.

Hack your biological clock

Take full advantage of what some call your 'biological prime time' (that is, the time of day when your energy levels are naturally at their peak). This isn't about being a morning or night person. You should – you must – be more precise than that. Specifically, your prime time is the moment of the day when your motivation and concentration are at their highest level. Figuring this out will help you determine when it's best to deal with important work, and when you're better off going for a coffee break. To determine your prime time, fill in the circadian rhythm assessment designed by researchers James Horne and Oleg Ostberg (Morningness Eveningness Questionnaire). The test takes ten minutes and can easily be found online, and determines your chronotype, or hours of peak alertness.

Once you've got the results, start building your schedule around them. If you're an early-morning person for example, move all your meetings to the afternoon and use mornings for the more demanding aspects of your workload.

Just so you know, none of the entrepreneurs we spoke to said they were more productive in the evening. On the other hand, at least 20 of them spontaneously spoke about an early morning start as one of the key secrets to improving productivity. First of all, the office is an incredibly peaceful place when there's no one else there, but more importantly, your mind is most lucid first thing in the morning, when sleep has cleared away mental clutter, leaving you equipped to tackle your most demanding to-dos.

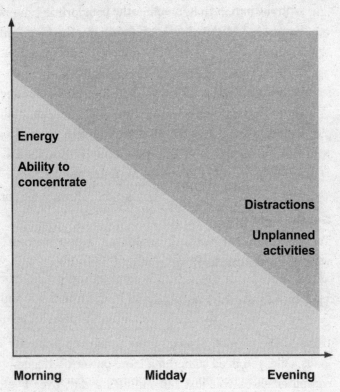

Try and establish an effective morning routine that makes the most of this clarity of mind. Don't ruin it by reading emails and filling up your mind with more junk. The entrepreneurs we spoke to all had a clearly-defined morning routine. Here are some of the most common recommendations:

> Define your three most important tasks. Then start with the hardest. (Remember the frog.)
> Exercise. 7 Minute Workout, anyone?
> Meditate. The best chance you have of not being disturbed is when everyone else is still asleep.
> Drink a big glass of water. You lose about 7oz of water during a night's sleep, which is not a lot, but it's never a bad idea to rehydrate yourself.
> Make your bed. A simple task easily accomplished will help provide motivation for those that follow.

Get the right gear
To create optimal working conditions, equip yourself with optimal materials.

That starts with your computer.

If the hourglass icon appears every time your computer loads a file, you need something more powerful. If a new computer saves you just ten minutes a day, over five years you'll have saved 25 days' worth of time. Surely that justifies shelling out $1,200 for a better laptop.

Mac or PC? Without wanting to lose friends, the large majority of entrepreneurs we met with work on Macs. The main reasoning is that they crash less often, and that they look better :) That said, most modern software is SaaS (which means you have access to whatever you need with any web browser) and as such is available for both Mac and PC. Your call.

Another useful tip we were given was to increase the tracking speed of your mouse. It might seem trivial, but it may change your life! If you use a mouse, try increasing its tracking speed to 80 per cent (100 per cent if you're feeling brave). It'll seem a little out of control at first, but after a few minutes' practice you'll get the hang of it. And if you use a trackpad, the rule of thumb is this: if you run your index finger diagonally across the pad, the cursor should easily cross the whole screen.

Also, keep a pair of headphones readily available. You'll have your hands free to take notes if you're on the phone (which also means less neck pain).

The last little thing the entrepreneurs suggested was to double up on all your cables and chargers, keeping one set at home and one at the office. They'll be easier to find and you won't waste time trying to remember where you last had them ... plus, your bag will be lighter.

Google is king

As far as software goes, you're better off taking your cue from the crowd. Google enjoys the dominant position in the marketplace, which means they can hire more developers, all of whom work non-stop to ensure their products remain cutting edge. And as one of the entrepreneurs we met with put it (quite accurately): Facebook was invented to take up time, and Google was invented to save it.

99 per cent of the entrepreneurs we asked use Gmail for email and Chrome as their web browser. Apart from being faster, the biggest leg up Google has over the competition is in the thousands of useful extensions it offers, which we'll go into more detail about in the pages to follow.

In the same way that Microsoft Office (Word, Excel and PowerPoint) revolutionized the way we worked in the 1990s, today's entrepreneurs have all switched over to Google's online solutions (Google Sheets, Google Docs and Google Slides). These tools boast three distinct advantages (on top of being free).

> Collaboration. Being able to work simultaneously and edit the same document in real time is a massive advantage: no more wasting time sending emails back and forth with large attachments. To write this book, the three of us worked exclusively on Google Docs.

> Save Automatically. No more worrying about losing your work when your computer crashes or trying to remember which file is the right one. Google saves your work automatically and allows you to access previous versions in your history. This comes in super handy when, say, the new intern accidentally deletes your whole document.

> Functionality. In addition to having all the same capabilities as Office, Google's tools also boast several unique functions[12] along with more sophisticated graphics (Google Sheets).

Microsoft retaliated by developing the Office 365 suite, which on paper offers a similar experience to Google's online solutions. In reality, the online features are still limited. But if your IT department doesn't give you a choice and requires you to use Office 365, it can do the trick.

---

[12] Google Sheets examples: The 'Unique' function returns unique rows in the provided source range, discarding duplicates. The 'Filter' function returns a filtered version of the source range.

If you're not sure which software to choose ...

As we said before, when in doubt about software, follow the crowd. When choosing a tool, pick the one that has the most developers working on it, which you can figure out by seeing which one has the most users. An easy way to do this is by checking out Google Trends (https://trends.google.com) before you make your choice. Below is a graph taken from Google Trends comparing the four main e-commerce platforms since 2004.

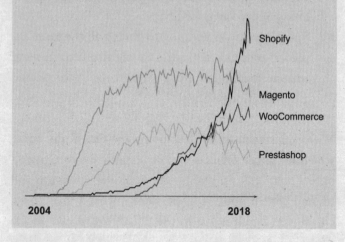

AUTOMATION: AUTOMATE REPETITIVE ACTIONS

The Golden Rule: if you need to repeat the same action more than *one single time*, automate it. Below are four areas in which automation is extremely simple.

Let your computer autofill forms

We've all been there a hundred times: spent ten minutes filling in personal details only to have the site crash, tried five different passwords before finally clicking 'Forgot Password', been forced to go credit card hunting just to buy something ... Online forms are a scourge upon the web.

However, there are some fantastic digital tools available which automatically fill in your details online (in addition to improving security). For remembering usernames and passwords, 1Password works well. If you're looking for something more comprehensive that'll fill in all your details, Dashlane was the one most-often recommended by the entrepreneurs we spoke to. And these tools work on your smartphone, too!

The only thing you'll have to remember with these tools is your master password – the open sesame for all your accounts on the web.

Let your computer sort through your emails

The emails you receive contain a wealth of information (recipient, subject, date, etc.) all of which can be used to automate responses and in turn, make your life easier. Gmail and Outlook let you set up plenty of automatic filters. Here are a few examples of what you can do:

> Highlight emails you receive from your boss and your five key clients with a red label, allowing you

to differentiate your most important emails from all the others.

> Automatically reply to certain emails. For example, if you receive frequent internship requests that you're unable to fulfill, you can set up a filter so that any emails containing the subject 'internship' sent from an outside email address will be met with an automatic response kindly turning them down. (This function is available under 'canned responses' in Gmail settings or select 'Reply with a template' when setting up your rule in Outlook.)

> Automatically delete or archive certain types of unnecessary emails. For example: attendance confirmations (i.e. emails with 'Invitation Accepted' in the subject line). You only need to know about declined invitations, not confirmed ones.

Mixmax = Gmail on steroids

Mixmax is one of only two tools that has its own box in the book, and for good reason. Mixmax can unleash Gmail's full potential, and was cited as a game changer by many of the entrepreneurs we spoke to. Here are a few of its main features:

1. Send later. You can set Mixmax to send an email at the date and time of your choice (for example if

it's the end of the day, and you don't want to irri-
tate your coworkers).

2. Set Reminders. Mixmax can send you a reminder
   if you haven't received a response to an email after
   a specified number of days' time, ridding you of
   the burden of remembering to follow-up yourself.

3. Share Availability. With one click, you can make
   any available gaps in your schedule visible to
   someone and then create an invite in both your
   calendars. This is an invaluable resource when
   it comes to scheduling meetings and preventing
   pointless, back-and-forth emailing.

4. Tracking. Mixmax lets you know if and when
   someone has read your email. Handy if you want
   to know whether to chase the person up or not –
   or are just curious.

5. Sequences. Mixmax allows you to mass email
   hundreds of your contacts at the same time, and
   then if they haven't responded within an allotted
   time frame it can follow them up for you with a
   personalized message. For example, you could
   write, 'Hey _____, I noticed you haven't replied
   to my email yet and wondered whether you needed any more information.' If you want to be a wise
   guy, you might even just type 'bump' or 'ping'. It's
   a little unexpected and will probably up your response rate.

Basically, you hit 'send', sit back, and let Mixmax do the work. The free version lets you use each function roughly ten times per month, which is pretty good to start with. Only the mail merge function isn't included in the free version, in which case you could always use Yet Another Mail Merge, a less feature-heavy, but still pretty solid alternative.

Let your computer handle processes

Many of the processes we use in our daily lives are based on conditional if-then statements (if x occurs, then do y). For example, if you receive your monthly invoice from a supplier, then you should first email him or her acknowledging receipt of said invoice, then file it away in Dropbox – a tedious, repetitive action that can easily be automated to save time and energy. One of the entrepreneurs we spoke to had successfully automated over 50 of these day-to-day processes.

The king of automation tools is Zapier, which can connect over 1,000 apps (including Gmail, Google Sheets, Outlook, Expensify, Dropbox and Facebook) to automate your work and boost productivity. Using the example of the supplier invoice, you could use Zapier to define emails from your supplier containing an invoice as the trigger, and then sending a response and filing the invoice in Dropbox as the resulting action. There are thousands of possibilities to explore (e.g. automatically blocking out the two hours before and after a flight in your calendar to account for transfer time).[13] An alternative to Zapier is Integromat, which has a more visual 'drag and drop' interface and some find it even more complete and powerful than Zapier.

Another tool we recommend is Hazel (currently only available for Mac, but check out DropIt for PC). Instead of connecting different services, Hazel automatically organizes files on your computer according to certain parameters you set. A basic example: if one of the documents in your downloads folder is larger than one gigabyte and hasn't been opened for over two weeks, Hazel can automatically delete it. Or, if a document contains the word 'invoice', Hazel can create a copy, rename it with the date and time, and automatically file it in your accounts folder.

If you're looking to take connectivity to the next level, then IFTTT (If This Then That) is worth checking out. It performs some of the same functions as Zapier, but also allows you to connect household devices. This is where it gets really interesting: you can water your garden automatically if it hasn't rained in a while, get an alert on your smartphone if you've left the fridge door open, turn

---

[13] The word *flight* appearing in your calendar acts as the trigger and the resulting action is automatically blocking two hours before and after the flight under the heading 'Airport transfer'. We recommend you add 'Invitation generated with Zapier' so that those accessing your calendar know it might not be 100 per cent accurate.

off the heating at home once everyone's left, put your phone on silent when you step into the office ... Essentially, you can pretty much *automate your entire life*. It's up to you to decide whether you find this cool or creepy.

If you use applications specific to your business that can't be linked up with Zapier or IFTTT, your best option is RPA (Robotic Process Automation). Instead of using computer code to connect up your applications (the famous API), RPA mirrors human behavior by observing the user perform a task, and then repeats those tasks, whether that be in comparing data or filling in forms. RPA is rapidly becoming big business with industry 'unicorns' such as UiPath or Blue Prism, which were valued at over a billion dollars at the time of writing.

We should point out that there's massive growth potential for automation in paper-heavy sectors such as banking, insurance and telecommunications. Robots would allow for the automation of everything from drawing up contracts, to claims management, to invoicing, to fraud protection. The main goal is to eliminate tedious tasks, thus leaving your workforce free to concentrate on tasks that stand to benefit most from their particular talents, empathy or judgement. Of course, most businesses could put specific software in place to take over these tasks, but the benefit of RPA is that it doesn't require a complete overhaul of your IT system, making it much cheaper in the long-run.

What can RPA do for you? If you find your daily tasks are becoming too repetitive, nothing is stopping you from putting in place your own RPA system. You don't need an IT expert; RPA doesn't require knowledge of coding. All you need is patience and common sense. On top of that, UiPath, for example, is free for companies with less than 250 employees.

Use AI

From *2001: A Space Odyssey* to *Blade Runner* and *Wall-E*, Artificial Intelligence has flourished on cinema screens for years. In real life, AI's progress has been slow by comparison. Until recently.

Everything changed in 2010 with the introduction of deep learning (a model based on the way humans acquire knowledge), which revolutionized the AI learning process. For example, let's say you were working on training an image recognition AI. Instead of having to teach the algorithm that a cat is an animal with four legs, whiskers, and two ears, you just give it access to millions of pictures of animals and tell it which ones are indeed cats. This radical advance has been made possible by the exponential growth of online information (largely thanks to social networks and online media) that now provides AI with its educational resource.

The upshot of all this is a sudden acceleration in AI development which is rewriting the way we live and work.

Of course, we don't yet know what long-term effects AI will have on the economy and society – only that they'll be tremendous. For now at least, we can use it to our advantage to handle low-value tasks on our behalf.

Voice recognition

The image of the boss dictating letters to a secretary is now completely passé. We can speak at least twice as fast as the fastest typist can type, and combined with voice recognition, our ideas can be written out faster than ever before.

In May 2017, harnessing the power of deep learning, Google's AI voice recognition software achieved 95 per cent accuracy in transcribing voice to text – far superior to human transcription. Progress in this sector has been considerably fast: in July 2016, the accuracy rate for Google's voice recognition software reached 91.5 per cent. Cortana (Microsoft's equivalent) and Siri (Apple) have followed similar progress trajectories.

You speak faster than you write so if you're not already doing so, we recommend using voice recognition to dictate your smartphone messages, whether that be for texts, WhatsApp, or anywhere else. But avoid sending audio messages to your recipient because messages are still faster to read than to listen to.

Where voice recognition AI truly shines is in the connected speaker/home assistant sector. Whether you use Amazon's

Alexa, Google Home or Apple's Homepod, these systems offer incredible potential for improving your personal productivity. Vocal command software has done away with the need for a screen/keyboard eliminating yet more friction points between you and a given desire. The moment it occurs to you, you can play a song, book a taxi, add something to your shopping list or buy something online.

Obviously, these speakers are best used at home, as opposed to in an open-plan office. That said, there is Alexa for Business which allows you to create or join a conference call, adjust the lighting or even the temperature without ever leaving your chair or touching your keyboard.

Predictive text for your phone

Swiftkey is one of the most popular Apps for iOS and Android, currently installed on some 300 million smartphones worldwide, at the time of writing. By proposing three options just above the keyboard on your touchscreen as you type, Swiftkey can significantly reduce the time spent typing on your phone.

The accuracy of Swiftkey's predictions made a significant leap forward in 2016 when Swiftkey moved away from a model based on the statistic likelihood of one word following another and adopted a deep learning model whereby it was able to predict what you actually wanted to say. So if you'd just mentioned your Monday morning in a text message, and you subsequently typed 'I had', the Swiftkey would propose 'a good weekend' rather than 'a good time'. Essentially, it's as if the keyboard is doing all the thinking for you.

Translation

For a long time, we believed that machines would never be able to perform accurate, nuanced translations. We considered them incapable of understanding the organic nature of language, whether in its subtlety, irony or double-entendre. However, since its inception in 2016, deep learning has changed the game. Newer AI software translations are now superior to the majority of translations provided by non-native speakers.

As a direct consequence, the idea of language as a barrier between people is disappearing from written communications, (emails, chat, etc.) and the entirety of the internet is becoming increasingly accessible to people all over the world regardless of which language they speak. It is now just as easy to read an article in a Korean newspaper as it is in your local one. For once, despite investing heavily in translation technology, neither Google nor Facebook are leading the market. That honor instead goes to Systran, a deep learning-based translation program that has reached a degree of subtlety and detail previously considered impossible. The results are remarkable (try their demo version for free, just google it). Unfortunately, you have to pay to get access to the pro version, but if you're looking for something free, take some advice from our entrepreneurs and install the Google Translate extension for Chrome. It will automatically translate any words you highlight, and you can use it to translate any page of your choice by simply clicking the icon.

Organizing appointments

Going back-and-forth setting up a simple appointment or meeting can take up a disproportionate amount of time and energy. AI assistants such as X.ai, Claralabs or Julie Desk provide a neat solution to this problem. With X.ai for example, just CC Amy@x.ai into your emails and Amy will take care of scheduling, proposing both parties convenient time slots according to availability. Amy will even suggest your favorite restaurants if you need to organize a business lunch. AI-powered virtual assistants cost anything from $20 to $200 per month depending on the level of service you are getting. Many of the entrepreneurs we spoke to said that the amount of time they saved as a result made those virtual assistants well worth the investment.

The future of AI

This is just the start of the revolution. Over the next few decades, Artificial Intelligence will take over more and more of these kinds of low value, time-consuming tasks. Startups are already looking at ways to exploit this. A startup called Growbots is developing AI to prospect for new clients so you don't have to. The introduction of autonomous vehicles will mean that we no longer have to spend time driving ourselves around. Instead we'll have the time for other things: working, reading, watching a film, or simply staring out of the window. Alibaba founder Jack Ma predicts that thanks to AI, we'll be working four-hour days and four-day weeks within 30 years. By then, the emphasis will be on the creativity we bring to a role and the quality of the work we produce rather than on the number of hours we spend working.

SPEED: GET THROUGH YOUR DAILY TASKS FASTER

To determine what impacts your productivity the most, you need to first figure out how you divide your time between tasks within a given week. How much time do you spend in meetings, on Excel, checking emails, or browsing social networks? If you're looking for a precise calculation rather than a rough estimate, you could use a free app like RescueTime, which runs in the background on your computer and smartphone and tracks how much time you spend on websites and apps, providing you with a comprehensive breakdown of your day. If you can't measure it, you can't improve it!

Write faster

We'd like to start by making an obvious point that lots of people seem to forget: at work, the only advantage your phone has over your computer is that you can use it easily as you move around. In everything else, your computer has the advantage. It's faster, more powerful, has a bigger screen and a better keyboard. In short, avoid touching your phone at work except if you're making a call!

Think of your phone as a kind of modem for your computer that allows you to communicate via text message or WhatsApp. When you're at work, leave it in your jacket pocket and don't use it! There are plenty of well-designed websites or desktop apps that allow you to access your phone from your computer, including WhatsApp (https:// web.whatsapp.com), Android Messages for web (https:// messages.android.com) or the Airdroid app (for iPhone users).

Type faster

First things first: let's test your typing speed (there are plenty of sites for this, but 10fastfingers is good). If you type less than 30 words per minute, you're slower than average – so the good news is that there's plenty of room for improvement. Just to give you an idea, a professional typist can produce between 70 and 100 words per minute, and the world record (held by Barbara Blackburn) is 212 words per minute (although she did have a special keyboard).

The secret to being a good typist is in the positioning of the hands on the keyboard. Your fingers should be able to reach all the keys with minimum movement. On a QWERTY keyboard, place your index fingers on the F and the J keys, which both have a little bump on them to help you find them without looking (yup, that's what they're for). Place your other fingers over the A, S, and D keys on the left and K, L, and ; on the right, with your thumbs resting on the space bar. From here, each finger corresponds to a specific zone of the keyboard (for example, your left ring finger should always be used to touch the W, S and X keys).

There are some great online tools to help improve your typing. For us, one of the best is Typingclub, which is used by over 50,000 schools across the United States. Try a ten-minute session each day, but be aware that typing speed follows a J-shaped curve – that is, changing your technique will make you slower to begin with, but you'll enjoy a rapid acceleration within a week or two.

Shortcuts to write faster

When you write an email, you'll often find yourself repeating certain phrases, e.g. 'our offices are located on 248 Acceleration Avenue, Westchester, New York.'

The way to bash that out faster than a hacker from Anonymous: Google Chrome's Auto Text Expander extension, which lets you assign pre-written sentences or phrases to particular shortcuts, such as ':addr' for your work address, then … presto. You could also try the aText App which costs $5, but which allows you to replace shortcuts across your entire Mac or PC as opposed to just on Chrome. There's also the Alfred app whose paid version does the same thing.

Here are a few shortcuts worth trying:

> Your professional and personal address
> Niceties used to start and end emails
> Your full name
> Your phone number
> Your bank account number
> Your passport number/driving licence details
> Your business details, name, web address, company registration number, tax ID ...
> Any phrase you find yourself repeating in your line of work, such as for making a business proposition, providing a quote, sending an invoice, proposing an interview or meeting, turning down an internship request, etc.
> Dynamic shortcuts such as today's date

Use templates

Canned responses allow you to insert pre-written content into your emails – a fantastic resource if you often find yourself sending the same emails over and over again. With canned responses, you can quickly tailor pre-written emails to individual recipients, saving you both time and energy. Gmail users simply need to set it up first in their Gmail settings. Outlook offers a similar functionality, you will need to compose a new email and click 'save as template' to make it a canned response that you will be able to use at a later time.

If you ever need to send identical emails to different people, personalizing just names and addresses, use Mail Merge. Basically, it combines a pre-written email with a spreadsheet of contact details that fills in the variables. For Gmail users, Mixmax does this very well, but if you're looking for a cheaper (not to mention free) option, Chrome's Yet Another Mail Merge (YAMM) extension does a good job. Outlook users, Yesware is the tool you need to do exactly that.

An example of a template might read: 'Dear << First_name >>, We are writing to confirm that our book has been published, and the launch party will take place on September 1st. We'd be delighted to also invite all your colleagues from << Company_name >>. Please let us know if and how many of you would like to come. Thanks and take care!'

Four ways to speed up communication by email

When it comes to communicating by email, the biggest threat to productivity is email ping-pong:

> Email 1: Here's the latest financial reporting.

> Reply: Great, what would you like me to do?
> Email 2: Check it over and write in any suggestions.
> Reply: Directly in the spreadsheet or via email?
> Email 3: Whatever you prefer!
> Reply: There's a mistake on the last calculation, and I think the table should be easier to read.
> Email 4: Here's the updated version, what do you think?
> Reply: Looks good to me.
> Email 5: Excellent, can you send it to accounting and CC me?
> Reply: I'm on it.

Once again, it's worth putting in some effort at the outset in order to avoid wasting it like this later on. Try these four simple techniques and you'll never look back.

1. Explain clearly at the beginning of each email exactly what it is you expect from the person you are writing to, ideally with a single, precise question.

The TL;DR technique is a handy way of summarizing a text that is too long or dense. At the top of every email, provide an extremely succinct summary of what your email is about. If you wanted to propose a training session to your colleagues, you could write 'TL;DR: Public speaking training next

Wednesday, let me know if you're interested', writing out the specific details underneath. (The abbreviation TL;DR stands for 'Too Long; Didn't Read' and is used on sites like Reddit to provide concise summaries of long texts.)

2. Structure your email precisely. Try the 'If ...Then' structure (© Tim Ferriss). So using the above exchange as an example, you'd write something like, 'Here's the proposed financial reporting, if it's good for you, send it straight to accounting and CC me. Otherwise, please indicate any changes or suggestions at the bottom.' By writing out one explicitly clear email, you avoid the need for a back-and-forth conversation.

3. Prioritize key info using bullet points, or better still, use a numbered list so you can refer back to specific items throughout the body of your email.

4. Sometimes, illustrating your point using images, graphs, and videos can be both faster and more effective than long-winded explanations. With one click, CloudApp lets you take screenshots of whatever you like (static images, gifs, videos, etc.) and lets you annotate them if necessary. Cloud App also lets you share access to the images via a copy-pastable link. In this case, the free version does pretty much everything you need.

Read faster

The average reader reads between 200 and 300 words per minute, but the fastest are capable of reading closer to 1,000 in that time. There are two key secrets behind their ability to read so quickly.

1. They don't subvocalize.

Subvocalization is essentially the process of mentally speaking the words we read, which slows reading speed down to speaking speed.

2. They increase their scanning speed.

Contrary to what you might think, our eyes do not read the words in a line of text in order, one by one, but in a series of five to six jumps, each one lasting about 0.25 seconds. To skim text faster, you can try reading the third word on each line and the third to last word on that same line, and let your peripheral vision do the heavy lifting.

The idea of doubling or even tripling your reading speed might seem highly appealing, and there are a number of books and sites that provide training. Legentas offers online lessons to help you reduce the number of stopping points on a line, while Spreeder trains you to read faster by flashing sequences of words across the screen, a method known as Rapid Serial Visual Presentation.

Despite the bold claims made by some of these sites, contemporary research suggests that there is in fact no magic formula. If we speed up our reading, our ability to remember and to understand is diminished as a result.[14]

Our advice is to try out fast reading techniques only on your longest, dullest documents. For everything else, we wouldn't recommend it. In fact, if you find yourself sitting by a fire with a good novel in hand, we'd even recommend slowing down.

That said, if you struggle to find the time to read, try listening to podcasts – or audiobooks. At least a dozen of the entrepreneurs we spoke to told us that this is the best way to make use of time while commuting, cooking, or working out. Podcasts cover a huge variety of subjects, from personal development, to news, to culture, and the best part is that unlike radio, you choose exactly what you listen to. Sure, the majority of what you learn won't be immediately applicable, but if there's one thing that the most successful people all have in common, it's their relentless thirst for knowledge, and boundless sense of curiosity. Warren Buffet claims to spend 80 per cent of his time reading, Bill Gates gets through more than 50 books a year, and Elon Musk claims he learnt how to build rockets simply by reading books. As former US President Harry S. Truman once said, 'not all readers are leaders, but all leaders are readers.'

---

[14] Keith Rayner, Elizabeth R. Schotter & Michael E. J. Masson, 'So Much to Read, So Little Time: How Do We Read, and Can Speed Reading Help?' *Psychological Science in the Public Interest*, 17 (2016): 4–34.

Improve your memory

Something that can take a crazy amount of time everyday is having to find stuff in our notes that we could know by heart: either lists of information (shopping, monuments you want to visit in a city, even a speech ...), or sequences of numbers (such as your building access code, credit card number, social security number, birth dates ...). You could in fact memorize it all.

You think you have a bad memory? Poor excuse: good memory is not an innate talent, it just involves learning and mastering some techniques, like any other subject taught in school. And frankly, it should be part of the syllabus in high school or college (especially for medical studies).

To remember unrelated things, such as a shopping list or a sequence of digits making a phone number, there's no point relying on your short-term memory. On average, your short-term memory lasts 18 seconds and allows you to store anywhere between five to nine pieces of information. If you want to permanently memorize information, you must use your long-term memory. We'll describe two techniques that can help you immensely with a little practice (and will also impress your friends and colleagues).

The first method dates back to antiquity: it is so effective that it is still used today (especially by memory athletes: yes, memory championships actually take place!). Orators back then could not use a printer or a teleprompter: to remember the key points of their speech, they used a technique known as the *memory palace*. The idea is simple: you imagine walking through a space you know well, such as your apartment or your childhood home, then place mental images in known locations that will remind you of the information to remember. Why does this work? Because this technique is based on a peculiarity of the human brain: our vast spatial memory, probably driven by evolution since our survival used to depend on our ability to orient ourselves in hostile environments.

Example. Here is the shopping list you need to remember: toothpaste, milk, cereal, paper towels, soap. Imagine the Statue of Liberty in New York. Look at the face of Libertas (yes, this is the name of the Roman goddess of freedom), her unsmiling face has broken into a toothy smile, her teeth are so white that it is surely thanks to a special kind of **toothpaste**. It's hot outside and Libertas' crown is failing to protect her from the sun beating down on New York, so she has placed several layers of red **paper towels** over her crown to help her cope with the heat wave. Look up again at her right arm which is stretching upwards: Libertas is having fun with her torch burning **cereal** flakes falling from the sky. Slowly lower your gaze and direct it towards her other hand, which is now horizontal to better hold a bar of **soap**. It's an olive-oil scented Marseille soap and the aroma is tickling your nostrils. Finally look down, the statue is no longer on a pedestal but her feet are standing in a pool of milk. Now restart from the beginning, imagine the Statue of Liberty again and redo the mental journey by viewing the five items on your shopping list. That's it: now you've got the gist of the memory palace method.

Did you notice that in addition to spatial visualization, we added colors, movement, smell and even the Manhattan summer heat? This is called 'synesthesia': it is a neuro-logical phenomenon where several senses combine, making it possible to memorize things much more effec-tively. Also remember that the wackier your images, the better you will remember them. This technique is infinite, and you can, for example, memorize the key points of an oral presentation by associating the items placed in your palace with the themes of your presentation. If you want to store information temporarily, you can re-use the same palace several times. But if your goal is to memorize something permanently, reserve a memory palace for only that list of information to avoid any mental confusion.

The second memory technique will allow you to remember sequences of numbers: building access code, credit card number, social security number, birth dates, telephone numbers of your loved ones ... This is the so-called major system method. It requires quite a bit of training at first, but once you realize what you get out of it, you will be pleas-antly surprised by your new ability and have a hard time doing without it! (And once you can remember the license plates of passing cars, you'll be ready to apply to the CIA).

Essentially, the major system consists of associating each digit from 0 to 9 with a consonant sound. The number 0 corresponds to the sound 'z' or 's' or soft 'c' (you can remember that 'zero' begins with a 'z'), the number 1 corresponds to the sound 't' or 'd' (you can remember that the letters 't' and 'd' have one vertical stroke each, as does the numeral '1') etc. Next you transform the numbers into words by adding vowels, for example '**dizzy**' for the number 10 ('d' and 'z') or '**date**' for the number 11 ('d' and 't'). Here are the number-sound associations and some tips[1] to remember them:

0 = 'z' or 's' ('zero' starts with 'z')

1 = 't' or 'd' ('t' and 'd' have one vertical stroke each, as does the numeral '1')

2 = 'n' (there are 2 vertical strokes in the letter 'n')

3 = 'm' (there are 3 vertical strokes in the letter 'm')

4 = 'r' (the letter 'r' is the last letter in *four*)

5 = 'l' (a left hand with the thumb stuck out looks like an 'l')

6 = 'j', 'sh', soft 'g', 'ch' as in cheese ('j' looks like 6 backward)

7 = 'k', hard 'c', hard 'g', 'q', 'ch' as in loch (you can draw a 'k' with two 7 characters)

8 = 'f', 'v' (a cursive lowercase 'f' looks like an 8)

9 = 'p' or 'b' (a 'b' looks like a 9 rotated 180 degrees; a 'p' looks like a backward 9)

---

[1] Hale-Evans, Ron (February 2006). Mind Performance Hacks.

You will remember words much more easily than an abstract sequence of numbers. If you want to remember November 7th, your nephew's date of birth, think about the day you saw him for the first time and imagine that he was drinking a glass of **sak**e ('s' and 'k' for 07) with his **d**a**dd**y ('d' and 'd' for 11) to celebrate his birth. You can of course make up longer stories to remember longer sequences of numbers. And if you want to go pro, you can learn 100 words by heart corresponding to the numbers from 0 to 99. By doing that, going from 'light' to 51 or from 51 to 'light' or from 'beef' to 98 and vice versa will be a breeze!

If you want to learn other techniques, we recommend the following book by Kevin Horsley, a master in the subject: *Unlimited Memory: How to Use Advanced Learning Strategies to Learn Faster, Remember More and Be More Productive*. But unless you want to memorize the order of cards in a deck of 52 cards, the two techniques we just shared with you should do the trick.

Mental maths – top five tricks

Mastering mental maths techniques does not only make you look cool (well, depends who you're talking to), but it can also save you time and help you calculate orders of magnitude quickly to make fast decisions. The good news is, you don't need to be a maths genius to do mental maths. You just need to learn a few tricks; you will find our top five below. And while some of these might seem trivial, we're ready to bet that you will still learn a thing or two.

Problem	Mental maths tricks
Figure out your 15% (or 20%) tip at the restaurant	Use the fact that 15% is 10% + 5%. Calculate 10% of the bill, then take half of that number and add this amount to the original 10%.
	> Imagine that your restaurant bill came to $50 and you want to leave a 15% tip. Start by calculating 10% of $50, which is $5 (we know you knew that :)). Now, cut that number in half and you get $2.50, which is 5% of the bill. Add up the two numbers to get to your tip amount: 5+2.5 = $7.50. Hence, your total amount due is $57.50 (50 + 7.5), which you might want to round up to $58, unless you're fine with carrying change.
	Now, if you are more generous and want to leave a 20% tip, think of 20% as being 10% multiplied by 2.
	> On that same bill of $50, 10% of $50 is $5, then double that amount, which is $10. Voilà, this is your tip.
Split the restaurant bill	Now that you've added in your tips, you might wonder how to split up that bill.

	Party of 4 > Say you're a party of 4. The easiest way to split up the bill is to cut that amount in half, and cut it in half again. Remember the total amount of your bill including tips was $58? Start by cutting $58 in half, which is $29. Now cut $29 in half again. And there you go, each person owes $14.50. We're guessing you didn't eat at a high-end French restaurant! Party of 5 > Dividing by 5 is the equivalent of multiplying by 2 and then dividing by 10 (you can also divide by 10 first and then multiply by 2). If the check amount is $58, then double that number and you get $116. Then divide that amount by 10, which is $11.60. For parties of 3 or 6 or 7, we're sorry but we don't have any hacks to share with you: you will need to do the division in your head. You can also use the calculator in your smartphone or rely on your friends to come up with the solution.
Estimate your driving time	Miles per hour If you drive on a highway, your average speed in most countries will be around 60 mph (the highway speed limit might be higher but you need to factor in the time to drive to the highway and from the highway exit to your final destination). And that's very good news, because there are 60 minutes in one hour! Therefore,

	1 mile = 1 minute of driving time. You want to drive from New York to Boston (95 miles)? That will take you about 95 minutes, or 1 hour and 35 minutes. Kilometers per hour In km/h, the average car speed on the highway is about 100 km/h. It's therefore much easier to estimate driving times. You want to drive from Hamburg to Berlin (300 km) ? You'll need 3 hours.
Calculate X% of Y	In some circumstances, you might want to calculate the VAT amount, say by applying a VAT rate of 6% on a total amount (before VAT) of $50. While calculating 6% of 50 might seem challenging at first, here's a little hack: 6% of 50 is equal to 50% of 6. And suddenly the result, which is 3, is much more obvious. You just need to remember that X% of Y is the same as Y% of X. Here's another example: if you need to work out 4% of 80 in your head, just flip it and do 80% of 4, which is much easier.
Guesstimate	We've been taught in school to figure out the exact answers to maths problems. In real life however, it's much more useful to come up with ballpark estimates instead. This is where guesstimates come in, they are a combination of guesswork and calculations. Here's an easy addition guesstimate. If you're buying groceries and you want to estimate how much in total you

will pay for 3 items whose prices are $10.20, $5.10 and $23.80, just forget the decimals and add up the numbers. In this example, add $10 + $5 + $23, which makes $38. That already gives you a ballpark figure of how much your groceries will cost you. Now, given that you have rounded down all numbers by eliminating the decimals, you know that you are underestimating the total amount of your groceries by an average of $1.50 (since there are 3 items with an average underestimation of $0.50 each). If you wanted to improve your guesstimate, you can add $1.50 to your initial guesstimate of $38, hence $39.50. That figure is closer to the exact amount in this example which is $39.10.

MAKE THE MOST OF SHORTCUTS

It takes as much time to drag the cursor across the screen and click on a link as it does to use three or four keyboard shortcuts. Unless you are a graphic artist or an architect working largely with visual software, use your mouse as little as possible. You'll quickly realize how much you can do without it. (Investment banking firms encourage new recruits to work without a mouse from day one.)

Taking the time to learn keyboard shortcuts is one of the most useful time investments you can make. In the box below, you'll find some key shortcuts that we recommend incorporating into your daily routine one at a time.

Gmail and Outlook shortcuts

Gmail and Outlook can be operated entirely with shortcuts. For Gmail users, simply select 'Keyboard shortcuts on' in the Settings menu to get started. Here are our top five:

The 5 Most Popular Gmail Shortcuts

Compose/reply	Compose **C**	Reply **R**	Reply to all **A**
… and forward/send	Forward **F**	Send (Mac) **⌘ ↵**	Send (PC) **Ctrl ↵**
Select and archive	Select **X**	Archive **E**	
Go to next/previous email	Previous **J**	Next **K**	
Go back to inbox view	With filters **U**	Without Filters **G I**	
Move the cursor to the search bar	**⇧ /**		

The 5 Most Popular Outlook Shortcuts (for PC)

Compose/reply	compose **Ctrl ⇧ M**	reply to all **Alt H R A**	
… and forward/send	forward **Alt H F W**	send **Alt S**	
Insert a file	**Alt N A F**		
Switch to different view	Email **Ctrl 1**	Calendar **Ctrl 2**	Contacts **Ctrl 3**
Go to the previous (next) message	Previous **Ctrl ,**	Next **Ctrl .**	
Search for an item	**Ctrl E**		

Google Sheets and Excel shortcuts

Unless you have plenty of time to waste, a mouse has absolutely no business whatsoever hovering around your spreadsheets. Google Sheets and Microsoft Excel share 80 per cent of the same keyboard shortcuts, making it easy for Excel users to switch to Google's online variants.

Here are ten Google Sheets/Excel shortcuts listed according to frequency of use. For our research, we asked those capable of putting together a spreadsheet with seven tabs in less than 15 minutes ... (Most were bankers and consultants.)

The most useful key according to our research is F2. In certain consulting companies, new hires are even advised to remove the F1 key so as to avoid bringing up the Windows Help menu when they were actually trying to hit F2. The F2 key allows you to toggle between Edit mode and Enter mode. If you're navigating across the spreadsheet, hit F2 when you've settled upon a cell, and the cursor will show that you're now editing its content. The left and right arrow keys will then move within the formula as opposed to continuing to move you around the spreadsheet.

If you use a Mac, you'll need to define the F-keys as 'standard function keys', otherwise you'll have to keep pressing fn and F2 simultaneously. To do this, go to System Preferences > Keyboard > Shortcuts.

Top 10 Mac Shortcuts for Spreadsheets	Google Sheets				Excel			
Edit selected cell	F2				F2			
Make a reference absolute or relative ($)	F4				F4			
Expand a formula	**Down** ⌘ D	**To the right** ⌘ R			**Down** ⌘ D	**To the right** ⌘ R		
Paste value only	⌘ ⇧ V				⌘ ⌥ V	V		
… and paste format only	⌘ ⌥ V				⌘ ⌥ V	T		
Format as decimal	Ctrl ⇧ 1				Ctrl ⇧ !			
… and format as percentage	Ctrl ⇧ 5				Ctrl ⇧ %			
Insert comment	⌘ ⌥ M				⇧ F2			
Center align	⌘ ⇧ E				⌘ E			
Redo	F4 or ⌘ Y				F4 or ⌘ Y			
Select row or column	**Row** ⇧ space	**Column** Ctrl space			**Row** ⇧ space	**Column** Ctrl space		
Select cell range to the right	⌘ ⇧ →				⌘ ⇧ →			
… and below	⌘ ⇧ ↓				⌘ ⇧ ↓			

Top 10 PC Shortcuts for Spreadsheets	Google Sheets		Excel	
Edit selected cell	F2		F2	
Make a reference absolute or relative ($)	F4		F4	
Expand a formula	**Down** Ctrl D **To the right** Ctrl R		**Down** Ctrl D **To the right** Ctrl R	
Paste value only	Ctrl ⇧ V		Alt E S V	
... and paste format only	Ctrl Alt V		Alt E S T	
Format as decimal	Ctrl ⇧ 1		Ctrl ⇧ !	
... and format as percentage	Ctrl ⇧ 5		Ctrl ⇧ %	
Insert comment	Ctrl Alt M		⇧ F2	
Center align	Ctrl ⇧ E		Alt H A C	
Redo	F4 or Ctrl Y		F4 ou Ctrl Y	
Select row or column	**Row** ⇧ space **Column** Ctrl space		**Row** ⇧ space **Column** Ctrl space	
Select cell range to the right	Ctrl ⇧ →		Ctrl ⇧ →	
... and below	Ctrl ⇧ ↓		Ctrl ⇧ ↓	

Browser shortcuts

These are the most popular shortcuts for Chrome and other web browsers:

Top 5 Shortcuts for Web Browsers	Mac	PC
Open a new tab	⌘ T	Ctrl T
Close tab	⌘ W	Ctrl W
… and reopen tab (if closed by mistake)	⌘ ⇧ T	Ctrl ⇧ T
Move to next tab (on the right)	Ctrl Tab	Ctrl Tab
… and move to previous tab (on the left)	Ctrl ⇧ Tab	Ctrl ⇧ Tab
Move to next field (in a form)	Tab	Tab
Move the cursor to the search bar	⌘ L	Ctrl L

Word-Processing shortcuts (Word, Google Docs etc.)

The Top 5 Word-Processing Shortcuts	Mac	PC
Go to the end of a line	⌘ →	End
… and go to the start of a line	⌘ ←	Home
Jump from one word to the next	⌥ →	Alt →
Delete one word	⌥ Del	Ctrl Del
Paste text without formatting	⌘ ⇧ V	Alt E S V
Attach hypertext link	⌘ K	Ctrl K

Shortcuts for common apps

We aren't going to list out every shortcut ever invented, but nevertheless, here are a few useful ones that could really make a difference.

> Slack: ⌘ + K (Mac) and Ctrl + K (PC) to go directly to the channel or person you want.
> Insert emoji for Mac: ⌘ + Ctrl + Space (It's a little more complicated for PC users: click on the keyboard icon that appears in the bottom right of your screen in the taskbar. Once the virtual keyboard has launched, click on the smiley face beside the space bar and you'll see the emoji keyboard). Lots of people also suggested Rocket as a great emoji app for Mac.

To work faster, don't worry! Here's how

We tend to take our foot off the gas when we're afraid of making a mistake, like when we read the same email over and over again in case there's something wrong. To go faster, you just need to know how to go back in time.

> Gmail gives you the option to unsend an email within a specific period of time (5, 10, 20 or 30 seconds). Simply enable the 'Undo Send' option

> in the Settings menu. We suggest choosing the longest send delay possible (30 seconds); we doubt it will make a difference to your recipient.
> There's always the universal shortcut for undoing an action: ⌘ + Z (Mac) or Ctrl + Z (PC) (and ⌘ + Y (Mac) or Ctrl + Y (PC) to redo it if you were a little too hasty). Another really useful shortcut is ⌘ + Shift + T (Mac) or Ctrl + Shift + T (PC) which lets you reopen a tab you've closed by mistake.
> If you have to fill in a password you can't see, (i.e. *******), highlight it and type ⌘ + C (Mac) or Ctrl + C (PC) before you hit 'Log in', which will save you having to type it out again if you get one of the characters wrong.

FIND YOUR FILES FASTER

In real life, the best way to organize things is to arrange them using a method that makes them easy to find. For example, if you wanted to organize your vinyl record collection, you'd do it alphabetically or according to genre. In the digital world, this type of organization takes up a significant amount of time. Modern search functions are so powerful that you can find any file you need in less than a second: much better than trying to remember how you filed something away in the first place. Here's our advice on how to make your searches as effective as possible.

Searching for files

Forget trying to manually find things in Finder for Mac or Explorer for Windows. The fastest way of finding the file you're looking for is to use an instant search system. Type in the first few letters of whatever it is you need and hit Enter.

> For Mac you have two good options, Spotlight (pre-installed) or Alfred, both of which can be opened with the ⌘ + spacebar shortcut.
> On Windows, use the Cortana search function via the Windows + S shortcut, or try Wox if you're looking for something a little more customizable.

Of course, for searches to work properly, you need to make sure you name your files appropriately in the first place. The ideal method is to start with the date (YYYYMMDD) followed by keywords. For example '20181201_Draft_Productivity.pdf'. This will ensure files get listed chronologically, making them easier to find later on. The only exception is on Google Drive where old versions of documents are automatically replaced.

Searching for applications

Using your mouse to select an application from your dock on Mac or via the Start menu on PC is a waste of time. Your keyboard will always be faster than your cursor. The quickest way to find what you're looking for is to use an application launcher. Simply type the first few letters of your app's name into Spotlight or Alfred for Mac, and either Cortana or Wox for Windows, and you'll have it.

The same goes for your smartphone. Don't waste time scrolling between screens in search of something. On iPhone, you can simply swipe down on the home screen to access the search bar, and on an Android device, just type the first few letters of the app you're looking for into the Google search bar on the homepage.

If you do need to switch between screens, for example if you're copying data, you can use the keyboard shortcut 'Alt + Tab' for Windows or '⌘ + Tab' for Mac. Sometimes, you need two apps on screen at the same time – one on the right, one on the left. This is really useful if you happen to be dragging and dropping, or comparing two documents. Here's how to do it:

> Windows, as its name suggests, is really at the fore-front when it comes to managing windows. To work in split screen mode, simply drag a window to the edge of your screen. By dragging a window to the left, for example, it'll automatically fill just that side. Drag it upwards to fill the whole screen again.

> On Mac, click and hold the green button on the top left corner of your window for a couple of seconds, then click on another window to make the two appear side by side.

Searching for emails

Gmail users benefit from the backing of the world's most powerful and accurate search engine, so in most cases you'll find the email you're looking for with a few well-chosen keywords. However, from time to time, an advanced search might be in order. For example you can try the following searches:

> Search by sender and subject: 'from: paul.chef@ gmail.com subject: Rib eye Steak'
> Search by sender and recipient: 'from: paul.chef@ gmail.com to: me'
> Exclude words from your search by using '-'
> Look for an email containing an attachment by typing 'has: attachment'

In Outlook, advanced search is very similar. Invest time to learn the few search operators that will be useful to you daily, it will pay off quickly.

When writing an email, we recommend you take time to write a descriptive subject line in order to make finding it easier later on.

Alfred: The Productivity Ninja

Alfred is the only app after Mixmax that we felt deserved its own section. Several entrepreneurs claim they use it over a hundred times a *day*. Apologies to PC users: Alfred is currently only available for Mac, and we have yet to find a comparable app for Windows. Feel free to skip this section!

Alfred was created in 2010 by an English couple named Andrew and Vero Pepperell, who work hard to improve it year after year. Because of this, Alfred is a true ninja app, capable of saving you significant time on those frustrating micro-tasks that eat away at so much of the day. Given everything it can do, the $25 price tag (a one-time payment, not a yearly fee) is pretty negligible.

Some of Alfred's most popular features

1. Instant Searches

On Mac, Alfred can take over from Spotlight search. As with Spotlight, press ⌘ + spacebar, and then type in the first few letters of whatever it is you are looking for. The main advantage of Alfred over Spotlight is that Alfred prioritizes results according to how often you've opened them, which means that in the majority of cases, you'll only have to type in the first two or three letters, and it'll pull up exactly what you need.

2. Web Custom Searches

To find a copy of *The Extra Hour* on Amazon, you'd usually have to follow four steps:

1. Open your web browser
2. Open a new tab
3. Go to Amazon.com
4. Search for *The Extra Hour*

With Alfred, you can search any site directly from its search bar (⌘ + spacebar). Then, assuming you've set 'a' as a keyboard shortcut for Amazon.com, you can reduce the whole process to one simple step:

> Type 'a The Extra Hour'
> into Alfred's search bar.

Another advantage of this is that you are far less likely to be distracted by other things in your browser – like that shiny new email that's just come in …

Other examples:

> 'g The Extra Hour' => Opens Google and search-
  es for *The Extra Hour*
> 'i The Extra Hour' => Opens Google Images and
  searches for *The Extra Hour*
> 'wiki The Extra Hour' => Opens Wikipedia and
  searches for *The Extra Hour*
> 'rt The Extra Hour' => Opens Rotten Tomatoes
  and searches for *The Extra Hour*
> 'm Central Park, NYC' => Opens Google Maps
  and searches for Central Park, NYC
> 't ananas' => Opens WordReference (or Google
  Translate), and translates 'ananas' into English
  (it's French for 'pineapple', FYI)
> 'y Casey Neistat' => Opens YouTube and
  searches for Casey Neistat

Your options are basically unlimited. You can set up
Alfred for any site containing a search engine.

3. Snippets

This is another function that has the potential to
save you hundreds of hours. Alfred incorporates a
Text Expander similar to the one we mentioned in
the section on increasing your writing speed. Basically, you define set phrases and their corresponding

shortcut (such as ':addr' for your office address) and wherever you type it, Alfred will fill in the rest.

Alfred: the bonus features

> Create shortcuts for dynamic variables like the date or time. For example, let's say you're naming a file: you could simply type in ":date" and Alfred will fill in whatever the date happens to be that day, e.g. '2018-04-24'.

> You can also load pre-written lists from Snippets, such as a comprehensive Emoji list ⌘ from Alfred Emoji Pack. To find an emoji, you'd then simply press 👆 + Spacebar and type 's' followed by the first letters of the emoji you're looking for, and it's done. It eliminates a step from Mac's emoji shortcut ⌘ + Ctrl + Spacebar.

4. Managing your clipboard

This is one of those features you don't really imagine will change your life, but believe us, the second you start using it, you'll never go back. Example: you go to paste something and realize you've copied something else in the meantime. With Alfred, you can just type in a shortcut like ⌘ + ⌥ + V and pull up every text you've copy/pasted in the past week. Problem solved in half a second.

5. Workflows

Alfred lets you go even further with Workflows – additional features and shortcuts functions created by the Alfred community. Examples:

> Type 'pwgen' to generate a secure password. Search Giphy by typing 'gif' followed by whatever funny GIF you're looking for.
> Get today's weather forecast for your area by typing 'weather'.
> There are plenty of workflows to choose from, all of which you'll find easily with Google.

Searching the web

Google's Advanced Search functions can also be incredibly useful:

> Insert quotation marks to perform an exact phrase search, e.g. *'Save time to enjoy more'*
> Insert 'site:' to search inside a particular website, e.g. *'site: youtube.com TED talk top 10 time saving tips'*
> Insert 'file type' to search for a particular type of file, e.g. *'filetype: pdf'*
> Insert 'define' to define a particular word, e.g. *'define: streamline'*
> Insert 'or' to run a combined search, e.g. *'acceleration or productivity'*

It's also worth mentioning the Resulter extension for Chrome, which is likely to become one of the most-used tools in your digital toolkit without you even noticing it. Instead of clicking on search results with your mouse, Resulter lets you use the arrows on your keyboard to scroll through results and select the site of your choice. The time saved is roughly one second multiplied by the number of searches you do each day. We'll let you do the maths.

The ten digital tools productivity freaks simply can't do without (i.e. the ones most frequently mentioned by our entrepreneurs)

1. If someone you don't know contacts you with a business proposal, you might want to find out about them and what they do before you reply. Instead of wasting time sifting through LinkedIn, you can install a Gmail extension called Contacts+, which will instantly display their LinkedIn and social media information (photo, location, job title, past jobs ...) on the right-hand side of your screen. We haven't come across any equivalent for Outlook at the time of writing.

2. If you're looking for the email address of someone you don't know, enter their name and the

name of the company they work at into the Clearbit Connect extension for Gmail or Outlook. You can even find email addresses for some of the Dow Jones' leading CEOs. You get 100 free lookups per month which should be more than enough for most users. The catch for using this service is that you agree to give Clearbit access to your contacts, which gives you an idea of how it works ... If you can't find the email you're looking for via Clearbit, try Hunter. It searches for all the publicly available emails for a given company and uses them to work out the format, e.g. *firstname.lastname@company.com*.

3. When someone sends you a contract or document that you need to return signed, don't waste time printing it out, signing it, scanning it and sending it back. Open the document with Acrobat Reader or Preview for Mac and insert your signature (you'll have to digitize an image of it first, which your computer's built-in camera should be able to handle just fine). Of course, none of this is relevant if you receive documents via platforms such as Docusign.

4. If you find yourself wasting time clicking 'next' while browsing Google or Amazon results,

AutoPagerize solves your problem by transforming a site with lots of pages into a single scrollable one.

5. Use Expensify to slash the time you spend on expense reports in half. Whenever you receive an invoice via email, simply forward it to receipts@expensify.com, or if you have a paper receipt, take a photo and Expensify will digitally read it using text recognition software.

6. The One Tab extension for Chrome lets you close all your tabs with one click. You can also use it to close only a certain group of tabs, e.g. all tabs to the right of the active one.

7. Paste for Mac is the app that's revolutionizing the clipboard by saving your entire copy/paste history. Clipclip is the equivalent for PC.

8. Ditch your scanner. With apps like iScanner (iOS or Android) you'll be able to turn your smartphone into a mobile scanner with similar results. And scanners are now often integrated natively in the operating systems of smartphones (via the Drive application on Android, or Notes on iPhones).

9. What to check first – Gmail, WhatsApp, Messenger, Slack or Skype? With Rambox, the answer

> is straightforward: all of them at once. This is a
> fantastic app that brings all your messages to-
> gether on a single interface.
> 10. Ok, so they're not technically a digital tool,
> but noise reduction headphones are lifesavers
> when it comes to staying focused in an open-
> plan office.

SPEED UP MEETINGS

Most employees spend a significant portion of their time
in meetings. The precise amount varies according to your
role within a company, but roughly speaking its between
20 per cent for junior-level employees and 80 per cent
for those at the top. And yet no one actually *enjoys*
meetings. We complain about them constantly. And
rightly so: they're too long, too frequent, and in most
cases, a waste of our time.

Before you call a meeting, ask yourself whether it is
absolutely necessary. In the words of economist and
social theorist Thomas Sowell, 'the least productive
people are usually the ones most in favor of holding
meetings'. A meeting should always serve one of the
following purposes:

1. To make a decision that requires the opinion and
   agreement of several participants.

2. To brainstorm.
3. To make/deliver a difficult decision.
4. To get people pumped up and excited about a new project or brief.

In almost all other cases, an email will do just fine. If you really don't have a choice, here are a few things our entrepreneurs recommend to help you get the most out of your meetings.

MEETING RULES

0 Delay.

1 Screen.

2 pizzas.

30 minutes.

0 Delay

The meeting is supposed to start at 9am, but the project leader just stepped out to get a coffee and doesn't turn up until five past. The marketing manager has an impor-

tant email to finish and needs 'about ten minutes'.
Finally, the meeting starts – only for the project leader
to realize that he doesn't have the right cable for the
projector. He goes off in search of a new one. By the
time you actually do start, it's already 9.15 ...

Sound familiar? Sure, it's only 15 minutes – but it's 15
minutes times the six people sitting around the table,
each of whom will now have to make it up at the end of
the day. For the company, that delay will cost the business
15 minutes x 6 people, or 90 minutes of lost time. This
is the premise for Harvard Business Review's Meeting
Cost Calculator, which is pretty fun to play around with,
for the record. (Just google 'meeting cost calculator'). So
far, we have yet to find a neater solution to this problem
than to just make sure meetings start when they're actually supposed to. Every minute of lost time is multiplied
by the number of people in attendance. So if you're the
one who's running the show, make sure you're there 15
minutes early to deal with any technical problems: it
makes more sense for one person to lose 15 minutes than
for the whole team to lose 90. If you often give presentations outside your office, we highly recommend investing
in an HDMI/VGA/DVI adapter (these are the three types
of ports used by almost all TVs and projectors). Kiss your
connectivity woes goodbye.

If the problem is with people arriving late, nip the issue
in the bud with a suggestion we picked up from one of

our entrepreneurs. Once everyone has arrived, propose finding a more convenient hour to meet each week in order to accommodate those finding it difficult to arrive on time. You'll find that 99 per cent of the time, those present will assure you this one is fine, and will take extra care to arrive punctually the following week.

1 Screen

A meeting's biggest enemies are smartphones and laptops, so to combat this, we recommend a phone stack (where everyone places their phone in a pile in the middle of the table) along with a strict 'laptops-closed' policy.

2 Pizzas

Amazon founder Jeff Bezos came up with what he calls the Two Pizza Rule: basically, if your meeting requires more than two pizzas to feed the group, there are too many people in it. In other words, keep your meeting size to six maximum – four if you really like pizza. You can then share the minutes of the meeting detailing any decisions made with your other team members via email. If it works for Amazon, there's no reason it can't work for you too.

30 Minutes

You may have heard of Parkinson's Law, which states that 'work expands so as to fill the time available for its completion'. Its author, Cyril Parkinson, was referring to British public administration when he wrote it in the

1950s, but Parkinson's Law applies just as well to business meetings.

Your calendar proposes hour-long slots by default, but that doesn't mean that your meetings need to be an hour long. In most cases, a half-hour meeting is more than enough to make a decision. If you use Google Calendar, you can activate the 'Speedy Meetings' function which will end any 30-minute meeting five minutes early so you can get to your next appointment on time. For meetings that will take less than 15 minutes, try conducting them standing up around a high table. When standing, we tend to cut back on lengthy discussions.

That said, bear in mind that an effective meeting starts with a well-defined agenda. It's much like cooking: if the recipe isn't right, the dish won't work out no matter how many ways you make it. Here are a few good rules of thumb:

> At the start of every meeting, read out the agenda so everyone is clear on what the objectives are. Better yet, put the agenda directly into the invite. A meeting without a clear objective is like the third *Lord of the Rings* movie: it just seems to go on forever.
> Anchor your talking points to the overall objective. So instead of 'discuss client services', go with something like 'how can we improve our customer service over the next year?'. This will force you to finish the meeting with some concrete decisions made.

> Get easier-to-deal-with items out of the way first, and leave the more complicated discussions till later – otherwise you risk running out of both time and energy. A good example would be a creative brainstorm, which is best saved for the end.

Creative brainstorm at the end of the meeting	Creative brainstorm at the start of the meeting	
1st Topic = 20 min	Brainstorming session = 40 min	Topics covered during the meeting
2nd Topic = 10 min		
3rd Topic = 10 min		
Brainstorming session = 20 min = Remaining Time	1st Topic = 20 min	
	2nd Topic = 10 min	Not covered in the allotted time
	3rd Topic = 10 min	

1-Hour Meeting

> Avoid off-topic digressions by putting out an idea suggestion box or what some companies refer to as a 'parking lot' (a piece of paper or a whiteboard work, too). That way you keep the main conversation focused on the tasks at hand.

> By the end of the meeting, objectives should have been met, decisions made, and next steps (along with deadlines) clearly defined for each participant. And, you should be able to summarize all of this in three to four lines of text; no one needs a full page of meeting minutes.

TWENTY/EIGHTY RULE: 20 PER CENT OF EFFORT YIELDS 80 PER CENT OF RESULTS

In the late nineteenth century, the Italian economist Vilfredo Pareto observed that 20 per cent of English landowners owned 80 per cent of the country's wealth – a pattern that seemed to transcend not only geography, but history, too. He had just discovered the universal law for the distribution of wealth (now referred to as The Pareto Principle). Several decades later, the principle has proven applicable to several other areas of the economy: 80 per cent of sales come from 20 per cent of clients, 80 per cent of a factory's production problems are caused by 20 per cent of the machinery, and so on. Obviously, the ratio can vary slightly – from 70/30 to 90/10 – but you get the idea.

The good news is that this theory also holds true in non-economic contexts, like our day-to-day working lives. If 80 per cent of the effects are produced by 20 per cent of the causes, it follows that we should be concentrating most of our efforts on that 20 per cent. This runs totally counter to the general belief that any intense effort will result in the same payoff, that all clients bring in equal value, and that every day spent on a project will produce the same results. Realizing this can revolutionize the way you work. You've effectively been given permission to put aside 80 per cent of your less-valuable to-dos in order to concentrate on the 20 per cent that are really going to make an impact. Some examples of this in action:

> If you're taking an exam where two questions account for 80 per cent of the grade, ignore the rest of the paper and devote your time to answering those two as well as you can.

> If you're running a startup, put in a 20 per cent effort to get your product 80 per cent functional, then take it to market. By doing so, you'll get feedback from your first clients and you can start iterating. Don't bother spending 80 per cent of your time trying to squeeze out those cool-but-non-essential functions. As LinkedIn founder Reid Hoffman puts it, 'if you aren't embarrassed by the first version of your product, you've launched too late'.

> If you have to write a report or put together a presentation, focus on the 20 per cent that will have the most impact on your audience. For example, if you know that they'll be particularly receptive to one of

your arguments, build your report or presentation around that position and cut out the rest. Accept that you don't need it to be perfect; in reality, you just need to get the job done. You've got better things to do than fine-tune insignificant details.

Of course, in reality, when you're conscious of the fact that there's more you could do, it's hard to know when to stop. Force the decision by setting yourself 'unrealistic' deadlines. As we mentioned earlier, we gave ourselves a single weekend to write the first draft of this book. Having this constraint forced us to concentrate on the essentials and not get lost in petty details.

So for example, if you have to send off a complicated business proposal, block off an hour of your time and send it to your client once the time's up. You'll be amazed at your capacity to get right to the heart of the matter.

Done is better than perfect.

To-do list to 'Accelerate':

Here's how to accelerate your speed of execution.

> Make sure to take enough breaks in your day and do not feel guilty about having a real lunch break. A break isn't just time spent not working or being lazy, it is a fundamental requirement for improving efficiency and creativity.

> Make time to exercise and think about your diet. What you eat has a huge impact on your level of energy.

> Adapt your schedule to your biological clock. If you are a morning person, move your meetings to the afternoon to spend your mornings focused on performing tasks with higher added value.

> If you perform an action more than once, try and automate it. You can start by downloading apps that will fill out all forms and passwords automatically.

> You will always speak faster than you write: start using voice recognition to write your text messages for example.

> If you have a computer in front of you, stop using your smartphone. Smartphones are less powerful, slower and less convenient to use.

> Learn how to effectively type on your keyboard: if you type less than 30 words per minute, there's room for improvement.

> Assign pre-written sentences or phrases to particular shortcuts by using a text expander app. You might become faster than a hacker from Anonymous.

> Invest time to learn keyboard shortcuts. This might be one of the most valuable investments of your life.

> Stop searching for your files or emails by browsing the folders in which you stored them in the first place. Instead, use an instant search tool where you will only have to type the first letters of what you are looking for.

> Speed up meetings with the following rules: 0 delay, 1 screen, 2 pizzas and 30 minutes at most.

> Apply the 20/80 principle by setting yourself 'unrealistic' deadlines. Done is better than perfect.

Conclusion – what will you do with your extra hour?

Assuming you've taken this book's advice, you should find yourself with a few extra hours of time for yourself every day. How you spend that time is up to you.

The way we see it, you can convert your productivity gains into one of two things: money, or time.

Option 1: Turn your increased productivity into financial gain. This option is inevitable if you choose to stay on autopilot and do nothing to change the way you live. Over time, your workload will expand to fit the time you've allotted to it, you'll do more, grow your business faster, get promoted early ... Essentially, this is the option humanity has pursued since the Industrial Revolution (and with it, consumerism as a way of life). Historically, we have used our tremendous strides in productivity not to work less, but to earn and consume more.

And who doesn't want to live better? Increasing your income means you've got more cash to spend on nicer stuff, better vacations, and so on. And of course, all of that will make you happy. At least – that's how it was supposed to be.

The question of happiness is a complicated one. You may have heard about an enormous study carried out by Nobel Prize winning economists Sir Angus Deaton and Daniel Kahneman that claimed happiness peaks at an annual income of $75,000. To measure this, they first set out to evaluate people's subjective perception of happiness in relation to income. They posed the following question to 450,000 people between January and December 2009: '[on a scale of 1–10 where 10 represents the best possible life, where would you say] you personally feel you stand at this time?' The results showed that everyone's subjective *impressions* of happiness really did indeed increase in proportion to their wealth. So essentially, if your name is Elon Musk and your job is sending rockets into space, you'll perceive your life as better than average.

However, the story was quite different when the researchers, aiming to measure *actual* happiness, asked questions like 'Did you experience a lot of joy/pleasure/stress/anger/etc. yesterday?' or 'Did you smile or laugh a lot yesterday?'. They found that the level of *real* happiness also rose in proportion to income, but only up to about $75,000 a year,[15] after which point objective happiness (measured by asking people about their recent emotions) tapers off. Why? Because even if your name is Elon Musk, you're not immune to stress, and won't necessarily get to see your friends and family more often than others.

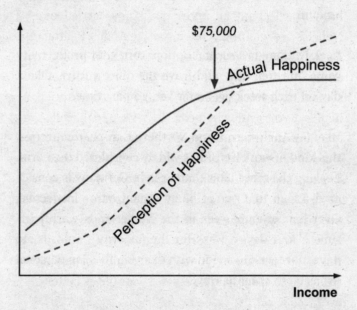

Of course, this $75,000 threshold is just an average, and won't hold true for everyone. The point is that to be

---

[15] Daniel Kahneman and Angus Deaton (Nobel Prize Winners for Economics), 'High income improves evaluation of life but not emotional well-being.' *PNAS*, 107 (2010): 16489–16493.

happy, you probably don't need to be earning as much money as you think. You really just need enough to look after yourself, enjoy a drink with your friends, and take a vacation every so often. Earning way more than that might get you a Maserati, first-class air travel, and stays in fancy hotels, but just know that none of that is likely to increase your *actual* happiness by any significant amount.

Luckily, there is a second option: turn your productivity gains into free time and leave the office earlier, take a day off each week or, better yet, go part time.

In many Anglo-Saxon and Northern European countries, this kind of work rhythm is widely considered the norm. Leaving the office later than 6pm in Germany is considered a sign that you're badly organized or ineffective. Over half of employees in the Netherlands work part-time – four days a week for the majority – in order to have more time to spend with their families, on personal projects, or volunteering.

It's also interesting to consider the historical perspective on the value of work. For a long time, society prized leisure over work. Most hunter-gatherer cultures only spent a few hours each day looking for food, so their working week was significantly shorter than ours (between

20–30 hours). During the classical period, work was considered a form of slavery; an affront to human dignity. Man, it was thought, must seek fulfillment through leisure above all else. The Romans similarly celebrated *otium*, time dedicated to meditating, reading, or nourishing one's social or political ambitions. In the Middle Ages, work was seen as divine punishment for man's original sin. Lords and knights preferred hunting, jousting, or competing in tournaments, regarding these activities as more honorable pursuits. Given, peasants and craftsmen did work long, hard days, but the abundance of religious festivals at that time meant that even they got to take it easy 90 days a year. And seeing as it was illegal to work by candlelight back then, they had no choice but to work part-time in winter. In fact, it was only following the first Industrial Revolution in the nineteenth century, when material gain became synonymous with happiness, that we began to see work as a good thing.

No one's dying words have ever been 'man, I wish I'd spent a little more time at the office'. When you learn to be ultra-productive at work, you also earn the right to not feel guilty about taking time to do what you love just for the sake of it: spending time with family and friends, working on projects you love, learning new things, volunteering … All of which won't necessarily make you rich, but will make you happier and help you to grow as a person. And who knows? If it helps, think of these activities as seeds you're planting that may one day grow into paid opportunities.

The future belongs to those who work less.

Resources

Below is a summary of the tools mentioned in this book along with a checklist to make sure you haven't forgotten anything. We promise that all are real recommendations, and that we haven't been paid to endorse any particular tools or apps.

Throughout the book, we've cited a bunch of very helpful tools. Now, productivity tools are evolving faster than the print rate of this book. If you can't find some of the tools we've mentioned here, it's probably because they have been replaced by more effective tools or have changed names. But we won't let you down, we are keeping an up-to-date list of tools at www.extrahourbook.com/tools.

STAY FOCUSED AND GET SH*T DONE BY ...

... Avoiding distractions:

> <u>Stayfocusd</u>, <u>Freedom</u> or <u>SelfControl</u> (free): Block your access to distracting sites (including Facebook) for a specified amount of time.

> Inbox when Ready for Gmail (free) or Boomerang – Inbox Pause functionality (free): Automatically hide your inbox so you can carry on with your work, write new emails and search your archive without getting distracted.

> Unroll.Me (free): Unsubscribe from all newsletters in a few clicks.

... Bookmarking stuff for later:

> Pocket (free): Saves all the web articles and sites you want to explore at a more convenient time and lets you access them from any platform.

... Creating an ideal environment:

> Noisli (free): Make any environment more conducive to focus by choosing from dozens of soundscapes, from trickling creeks to cabin thunderstorms.

SAVE TIME WHILE SURFING WITH CHROME EXTENSIONS

> AdBlock (free): Prevent ads and pre-roll videos from automatically loading and slowing your search engine down.

> Dashlane (free for the basic version): Remember one Master Password and let Dashlane take care of the rest, auto-filling forms, addresses, bank details, and passwords on your behalf.

> Resulter (free): Use the arrows on your keyboard to browse Google results faster.

> OneTab (free): Free up memory space by closing all open tabs with one click.

> The Great Suspender (free): Automatically suspend unused tabs to give you more memory space. Control which tabs are closed in the settings menu.

> AutoPagerize (free): Automatically turn websites with several pages into one long, scrollable one for more efficient browsing.

> Don't Fuck With Paste (free): Copy and paste even on sites where it isn't usually possible.

SPEED UP EMAIL

> MixMax (available for free or from $9 to $50 per month depending on which features you want): The ultimate productivity tool for Gmail. Send 'mail merge' campaigns, track your emails, use templates with shared access, schedule emails to be sent later, use Salesforce integration, automatically arrange meetings via your calendar ... The free version lets you use each function ten times per month, which is enough to get you started. Only the mail merge function isn't offered with the free version, but you can always use Yet Another Mail Merge for free instead. While YAMM offers fewer features, overall, it's still pretty good.

> Keep your address book up-to-date
  - <u>Contacts+ extension for Gmail</u>: Find and synchronize detailed contact information (including photos, social networks, etc.)

> Find any email address
  - <u>Clearbit</u> for Gmail or Outlook (free for up to 100 lookups per month): Find an email for someone simply by entering their name and that of their company.
  - If you can't find what you need through Clearbit, use <u>Hunter</u>. Hunter searches for any publicly-listed email addresses a business may have, and uses this information to figure out their format, i.e. firstname.lastname@company.com.

> Manage emails with Inbox Zero
  - Turn on Gmail keyboard shortcuts.
  - Enable the 'Send and Archive' function in the Gmail settings menu so that you can send and archive emails with one click.
  - Create email filters that automatically archive certain emails, such as meeting acceptance confirmations (except maybe from your boss – you'll want to know whether he or she is going to show up). Here's the filter you'll need: *from: -(boss@business.com); subject: (accepted:); has the words: *.ics; has: attachment; Do this: Skip Inbox, Apply label 'Accepted Invite'.*

– Automatically prioritize emails using labels. Apply a filter so that emails from your boss are automatically labelled VIP and are tagged in red: *from:* boss@company.com; *Apply label 'VIP'*.

MAKE USE OF TIMES WHEN YOU WON'T HAVE WIFI

> Google Drive Offline (free): Enable offline access in the Google Drive settings to use Google Docs, Sheets and Slides in offline mode when you're on a plane or there isn't an available internet connection.

AUTOMATE ANY MANUAL TASK THAT YOU'LL HAVE TO DO MORE THAN ONCE

> If your applications are compatible: Zapier (free or pro version for $20/month), IFTTT (free), or Integromat (basic plan is free)
> If you use very specific applications: UiPath
> Manage files: Hazel (only available for Mac with a one-off payment of $32) or DropIt (PC equivalent available for free).

MAKE YOUR LIFE A LITTLE EASIER

> Alfred App for Mac only (the search function is free, otherwise it's a one-time payment of $25): Run a search for a file or open an application without using

the mouse. Speed up typing using Snippets, access the clipboard quickly, or instantly run a search on any site with custom web searches.

> Swiftkey (free mobile app): Speed up your typing on a smartphone.

> 10fastfingers: Test your typing speed, then Typing-club to practice.

> CloudApp (free for the basic version, $25 per month for the full version): Create, annotate, and share screenshots or animated GIFs with just a few clicks. To share, you simply attach a hypertext link, which is ideal for email.

> aText or Auto Text Expander (one-time payment of between $5 and $35 depending on which version you choose): Speed up writing using shortcuts and abbreviations, e.g. '*addr*' to autofill your office address.

> Paste for Mac (free) or Clipclip for PC (free): Save your copy and paste history for easy access.

> Expensify: Create automatic expense reports. When you receive an invoice via email, simply forward it to receipts@expensify.com.

> iScanner (iOS ou Android): Create a quick, high-quality scan of any document with your mobile.

> Rambox: Group all your messaging, chat, and email apps into a single interface.

USE YOUR COMPUTER AS YOUR PHONE

> Android Messages (free, go to messages.android. com): Send text messages (SMS) from your computer instead of with your Android phone. Airdroid (iOS and Android) works well, too.
> Messages (free app for Mac): to send text messages (SMS) from your computer instead of with your iPhone.
> WhatsApp Web (free, go to web.whatsapp.com): to send WhatsApp messages from your desktop. Also available as a desktop app.

JOIN THE EXTRA HOUR COMMUNITY

> On Facebook: XHbook
> On Twitter: @XHbook
> On Linkedin: XHbook

Acknowledgements

We'd like to thank the 300+ entrepreneurs whose help made this book possible, but in particular we'd like to thank the following people (in alphabetical order): David Adamczyk, Deyola Adekunle, Maxime Alay-Eddine, Emmanuel Alquier, Pierre-Camille Altman, Omid Ashtari, Abhinav Asthana, Kelvin Au, Maxime Barbier, Julien Barbier, Thomas Barret, David Baruchel, Benjamin Bely, Emmanuelle Bersier, Florent Berthet, Mary Biggins, Camille Blaise, Hervé Bloch, Antoine Bolze, Tilo Bonow, Damien Börjesson, Alex Bortolotti, Dimitri Bosch, Alexis Botaya, Benoît Bouffart, Hervé Bourdon, David Boureau, Emmanuel Bourmalo, Augustin Bouyer, Cédric Boyer Chammard, Stan Boyet, Gavrilo Bozovic, Sebastian Brannstrom, William Brassier, Michael Bremmer, Antoine Brenner, Sylvain Brissot, Rose Broome, Geoffrey Bruyère, Stewart Butterfield, Julien Callede, Jérôme Calot, Sébastien Camus, David Cancel, Emilio Capela, Holly Cardew, Louis Carle, Sébastien Caron, Adelia Carrillo, Tom Carter, Franck Caudrelier, Damien Cavaillès, Thomas Ceccaldi, Jean-David Chamboredon,

Romain Champourlier, Lionel Chouraqui, Jérémy Clédat, David Cohen, Romain Cottard, Julien Coulaud, Xavier Damman, Aurélie Danglas, Robin Dauzon, Guillaume David, Kevin Davis, Abram Dawson, Augustin de Belloy, Godefroy de Bentzmann, Quentin de Colombières, Jean de La Rochebrochard, Cédric De Saint Léger, Louis De Vaumas, Cecilia Debry, Julien Decroix, Adrien Degouve, Florian Delifer, Alex Delivet, Tiffany Depardieu, Marc Désenfant, Philippe Desgranges, Grégoire Devoucoux, Jérémy Doutté, Adam Draper, Vincent Dromer, Antoine Dubois-Randé, Alexis Ducros, Sean Duffy, Florian Dupas, Manutea Dupont, Daniel Ek, Thibaud Elziere, Ryan Evans, Gilles Fabre, Adrien Falcon, Mary Fallon, Denis Fayolle, Jonathan Ferrebeuf, Antoine Ferrier-Battner, Ashley Finch, Florian Fine, Étienne Fischer, Sylvie Fleury, Stéphanie Florentin, Lucile Foroni, Tiago Forte, Nicolas Fouché, Benjamin Fouquet, Bruno Fridlansky, Jean-Charles Gabaix, Thomas Gabelle, Anh-Tuan Gai, Michel Galibert, Clayton Gardner, Antoine Garnier, Joshua Gartland, Antoine Gastal, Cédric Gaudard, Fabrice Gaumont, Olivier Gemayel, Anthemos Georgiades, Guillaume Gibault, Grégoire Gilbert, Ray Gillenwater, Kim Gjerstad, Alison Go, Olivier Godement, Tanguy Goretti, Michel Gotlib, Jeanne Granger, François Grante, Nick Gray, Matt Greener, Olivier Grémillon, Thomas Guillory, Daniel Ha, Kristen Hadeed, Laurin Hainy, Marie Hardel, Yan Hascoet, Benoit Hediard, Émeric Henon, Sean Henry, Calvin Hohener, Ryan

Hoover, Tatiana Jama, Baptiste Jamin, Benjamin Jean, Cyril Jessua, Karim Jourdain, Oliver Jung, Sylvain Kalache, Gil Katz, Anne Kavanagh, Laurent Kennel, Louis Kerveillant, Vahritch Kharmendjian, Graciela Kincaid, Geoffrey Kretz, Kevin Labory, Jessica Lachs, Quentin Lacointa, Margaux Lajouanie, David Lakomski, Thomas Lang, Marie Le Louarn, Antoine Leclercq, Tristan Legros, Stanislas Leloup, Alexandre Lemétais, Fabrice Lenoble, Ben Lerer, Arnaud Limbourg, Chris LoPresti, Ludo Louis, Aura Lunde, Mai Ly Nguyen – Terreaux, Riana Lynn, Robby Macdonell, Gautier Machelon, Thibaut Mallecourt, Nicolas Maloeuvre, Kevin Mamode, Cédric Mao, Justin Mares, Hadrien Matringe, Olivier Maurel, Nicole Mazza, Frédéric Mazzella, Melody McCloskey, Michelle McGovern, Claire McTaggart, Tom Mendoza, Jeroen Merchiers, Magali Mermet, David Micheau, Matt Mickiewicz, Paul Midy, Georges Mitchell, Vincent Moindrot, Gillian Morris, Axel Mouquet, Tomas Moyano, Max Mullen, Félix Mündler, Fabrice Nadjari, Vincent Nallatamby, Thomas Nanterme, Kris Narunatvanich, Dai Nguyen, Martin Ohannessian, Dominique Palacci, Nic Pantucci, Luca Parducci, Neil Parikh, Kathrin Parmentier, Christophe Pasquier, Jonathan Path, Thibaut Patouillard, Jean-Marc Patouillaud, Melvin Paz, Nilan Peiris, Vincent Pere, Charles-Alexandre Peretz, Tanguy Perodeau, Jean Perret, Laurent Perrin, Ben Peterson, Julien Petit, Michael Phillips Moskowitz, Mathieu Picard, Leonard Picardo, Anastasia Pichereau, Magalie Pigeon, Adam

Pittenger, Sam Plunkett, Antoine Porte, Charles-Henri Prevost, Nicolas Princen, Jeremie Prouteau, Yannick Quenec'hdu, Manoj Ranaweera, Naval Ravikant, Timothée Raymond, Francois Raynaud de Fitte, Navdeep Reddy, Mathieu Remy, Maxime Renault, Kévin Richard, Camille Richon, Adam Ringler, Kayla Roark, Julien Robert, Kevin Roche, Polly Rodriguez, William Roy, Ariel Rozenblum, Pierre-Emmanuel Saint-Esprit, Martin Saint-Macary, Baptiste Saintaubin, Ryan Sanders, Aurélien Schmitter, Erik Schünemann, Amir Segall, Sevak Sevak, Rubin Sfadj, Cedric Sisco, Pierre-Édouard Stérin, Alix Taffle, Tao Tao, Florent Tardivel, Chris Taylor, Michael Terrel, Yann Teyssier, Anke Thiele, Anh Tho Chuong, Benjamin Tierny, Cédric Tomissi, Hao Tran, Stephanie Trang, Mark Trevail, Olivier Trouille, Laurent Untereiner, Kathleen Utecht, Mikael Uzan, Antoine Van den Broek, Roxanne Varza, Arnaud Velten, Marc Verstaen, Antoine Vettes, Geoffrey Vidal, Jose Vieitez, Markus Villig, Sébastien Vollant, Thomas Volpi, Ryan Williams, Claire Wozniak, Eric Yuan, Alice Zagury, Benjamin Zenou.

We'd also like to say a huge thank you to all our proofreaders for their exceptional attention to detail, and above all their honesty (the 63rd draft doesn't look anything like the first!): Claire Wozniak, Romain Francoz, Alexandra Le Guiner, Jérémy Doutté, Jonathan Ferrebeuf, David Micheau, Julien Leynaud, Yannick Quenec'hdu,

Thomas Cambau, Philippe Desgranges, Flora Ganther, Sara Moarif, Simon Bennett, Liz Eavey, Deyola Adekunle. We'd also like to thank our fantastic translators Matthew Belsham and Danielle Courtenay for their awesome work and also their patience. If you enjoyed reading this book and feel that you've learned something along the way, please write us a review online: a little help is always welcome :)

About the authors
(Will, Bao and Jerome)

Will is co-founder of clothing brand Loom, where he advocates for a textile industry that is more respectful of people and the environment. Prior to that, he co-founded Merci Alfred, a male generalist media outlet. In these two professions, what he prefers is choosing slightly obscure subjects to make (very) long articles.

Bao is an investor in venture capital. He invests in innovative early-stage companies and he supports their founders in their growth journey. He was previously Head of EMEA at HotelTonight, the hotel booking app acquired by Airbnb. He has traveled the world, and is a passionate cook who regularly invites Top Chef contestants to dinner at his place in the hope of scoring a few tips.

Jerome is an expert in user experience. He helps give a second life to objects by improving the experience of Back Market customers, an online platform dedicated to refurbished tech devices. He previously co-founded One More Thing Studio, a French mobile app development agency. He went to his first Burning Man Festival when he was 23 and has backpacked his way around the world. Jerome now organizes Opal, a free annual festival in France, and in his spare time plays guitar, rides a motorbike and enjoys hanging around the more underground parts of Paris (literally).

If the pages of this book have helped you in any way, we'd be delighted to hear from you at hey@extrahourbook.com. You can also find us on Facebook, LinkedIn and Twitter by searching for 'xhbook'. We can also meet you and your colleagues in person: check out http://extrahourbook.com/conf.

extra
hour